Holt Literature and Language Arts
Fifth Course

Universal Access
Holt Interactive Writer and Speaker

HOLT, RINEHART AND WINSTON

ISBN 0-55-400267-1

ISBN 978-0-55-400267-5

7 8 9 10   1689   14 13 12 11

4500298600

Table of Contents

My Writing Workshops

Unit 1

Editorial

Unit 2

Short Story

Unit 3

Historical Investigation Report

Unit 4

Reflective Composition

Unit 5

Literary Analysis: Novel

Unit 6

Biographical Narrative

My Presentations

Unit 1

Presenting and Evaluating Speeches

Unit 2

Presenting a Story

Unit 3

Presenting an Investigation Report

Unit 4

Presenting a Reflective Composition

Unit 5

Presenting a Literary Analysis

Unit 6

Media Workshop: Analyzing Media

This Book and You

This book, *Holt Interactive Writer and Speaker,* accompanies the **HOLT LITERATURE & LANGUAGE ARTS** program and provides you with a variety of practice resources. These include Writing and Speaking Resources, My Writing and Speaking Records, My Writing Ideas, My Listening Notes and Speaking Ideas, My Writing Workshops, and My Presentations.

WRITING AND SPEAKING RESOURCES

These pages are designed as a reference for you. You can use the writing strategies, active-listening strategies, and effective speaking strategies not only in your English-Language Arts classes but also in all your other subject areas. Keep copies of these pages in your subject notebooks or laminate them and refer to them whenever you read or begin a major assignment.

California Content Standards and Correlations list the standards for achievement in Writing, Written and Oral Language Conventions, and Listening & Speaking adopted by the California State Board of Education. The chart shows you where each standard is covered in this booklet.

Proofreading Guidelines and Symbols should be used for all writing workshops in this booklet.

MY WRITING AND SPEAKING RECORDS

This set of forms helps you assess and organize your writing and speaking projects and set goals for future work.

You can use the forms in this section to record your work, to establish goals, and to think critically about your work in a variety of areas. These areas include writing, listening, and speaking. Use these forms to evaluate your work and to identify areas for improvement. Many forms can also be used to evaluate a classmate's work.

MY WRITING IDEAS

Use these graphic organizers to jot down ideas for all your writing projects.

MY LISTENING NOTES AND SPEAKING IDEAS

These pages give you a place where you can take notes while listening to your classmates' speeches and presentations. You can also write down your ideas for your own speeches and presentations.

MY WRITING WORKSHOPS

For each stage of the writing process, from Prewriting through Revising, you are given a chart or graphic organizer format to help you plan, organize, evaluate, and revise your work.

- **Prewriting** worksheets help you work through this step before you write your first draft.
- The **Prompts** page gives you ideas for what to write about, including writing ideas for careers and other school subject areas.
- A **Think Sheet** provides a format for you to evaluate the Student Draft in your textbook before drafting your own papers.
- A **Drafting** framework guides you through a plan to help you produce drafts that follow A Writer's Framework in your textbook.
- A form for **Peer- and Self-Evaluation** gives you the opportunity to rate your own writing or and your classmates' writing on the Guidelines provided in your textbook and to make positive suggestions for improvement.
- A **Revising** form gives you a rubric for analyzing a draft and identifying problems and solutions.

You have the opportunity with the **Sample Papers** to practice evaluating the writing of others, based on the **Framework** provided. **Practice with Conventions** helps you master common English language skills, such as grammar, punctuation, capitalization, and spelling.

MY PRESENTATIONS

Projects-Planning Guides and **Evaluation Guides** help you plan your work and evaluate both your own and your peers' finished projects. A **Think Sheet** gives you a format for evaluating the effectiveness of your projects and setting goals for future projects.

This Book and You

Writing and Speaking Resources

California Content Standards and Correlations

The California State Board of Education has adopted a set of standards for achievement in Writing, Listening, and Speaking. You will be expected to master these standards for your grade level during the school year.

Writing		
1.0	Students write coherent and focused texts that convey a well-defined perspective and tightly reasoned argument. The writing demonstrates students' awareness of the audience and purpose and progression through the stages of the writing process.	37–44, 50–58, 64–72, 78–86, 92–101, 107–114
1.1	Demonstrate an understanding of the elements of discourse (e.g., purpose, speaker, audience, form) when completing narrative, expository, persuasive, or descriptive writing assignments.	37–42, 44, 50–56, 58, 64–70, 72, 78–84, 86, 92–99, 101, 107–112, 114, 127-131
1.2	Use point of view, characterization, style (e.g., use of irony), and related elements for specific rhetorical and aesthetic purposes.	37–42, 44, 50–56, 58, 64–70, 72, 78–84, 86, 92–99, 101, 107–112, 114, 127-131
1.3	Structure ideas and arguments in a sustained, persuasive, and sophisticated way and support them with precise and relevant examples.	37–40, 42, 44, 50–56, 58, 64–70, 72, 79–84, 86, 92–99, 101, 107–112, 114
1.4	Enhance meaning by employing rhetorical devices, including the extended use of parallelism, repetition, and analogy; the incorporation of visual aids (e.g., graphs, tables, pictures); and the issuance of a call for action.	38–42, 44, 52–56, 58, 67–70, 72, 79–84, 86, 93–99, 101, 109–112, 114
1.5	Use language in natural, fresh, and vivid ways to establish a specific tone.	39, 41–44, 52–57, 67–72, 81, 83–86, 94–100, 109–112, 113
1.6	Develop presentations by using clear research questions and creative and critical research strategies (e.g., field studies, oral histories, interviews, experiments, electronic sources).	132-135
1.7	Use systematic strategies to organize and record information (e.g., anecdotal scripting, annotated bibliographies).	38–40, 51–53, 65–67, 79–81, 93–97, 108–109
1.8	Integrate databases, graphics, and spreadsheets into word-processed documents.	
1.9	Revise text to highlight the individual voice, improve sentence variety and style, and enhance subtlety of meaning and tone in ways that are consistent with the purpose, audience, and genre.	41–47, 54–61, 68–75, 82–89, 97–101, 110–113, 127-131
2.0	Students combine the rhetorical strategies of narration, exposition, persuasion, and description to produce texts of at least 1,500 words each. Student writing demonstrates a command of standard American English and the research, organizational, and drafting strategies outlined in Writing Standard 1.0.	39–44, 53–57, 66–71, 81–85, 96–100, 109–113

Writing and Speaking Resources

2.1	Write fictional, autobiographical, or biographical narratives: **a.** Narrate a sequence of events and communicate their significance to the audience. **b.** Locate scenes and incidents in specific places. **c.** Describe with concrete sensory details the sights, sounds, and smells of a scene and the specific actions, movements, gestures, and feelings of the characters; use interior monologue to depict the characters' feelings. **d.** Pace the presentation of actions to accommodate temporal, spatial, and dramatic mood changes. **e.** Make effective use of descriptions of appearance, images, shifting perspectives, and sensory details.	50–63, 78–91, 107–119
2.2	Write responses to literature: **a.** Demonstrate a comprehensive understanding of the significant ideas in works or passages. **b.** Analyze the use of imagery, language, universal themes, and unique aspects of the text. **c.** Support important ideas and viewpoints through accurate and detailed references to the text and to other works. **d.** Demonstrate an understanding of the author's use of stylistic devices and an appreciation of the effects created. **e.** Identify and assess the impact of perceived ambiguities, nuances, and complexities within the text.	40, 41, 45–47, 54, 55, 57, 59–61, 68–73, 75, 82–84, 86–89, 92–106
2.3	Write reflective compositions: **a.** Explore the significance of personal experiences, events, conditions, or concerns by using rhetorical strategies (e.g., narration, description, exposition, persuasion). **b.** Draw comparisons between specific incidents and broader themes that illustrate the writer's important beliefs or generalizations about life. **c.** Maintain a balance in describing individual incidents and relate those incidents to more general and abstract ideas.	78–90
2.4	Write historical investigation reports: **a.** Use exposition, narration, description, argumentation, or some combination of rhetorical strategies to support the main proposition. **b.** Analyze several historical records of a single event, examining critical relationships between elements of the research topic. **c.** Explain the perceived reason or reasons for the similarities and differences in historical records with information derived from primary and secondary sources to support or enhance the presentation. **d.** Include information from all relevant perspectives and take into consideration the validity and reliability of sources. **e.** Include a formal bibliography.	64–77
2.5	Write job applications and résumés: **a.** Provide clear and purposeful information and address the intended audience appropriately. **b.** Use varied levels, patterns, and types of language to achieve intended effects and aid comprehension. **c.** Modify the tone to fit the purpose and audience. **d.** Follow the conventional style for that type of document (e.g., résumé, memorandum) and use page formats, fonts, and spacing that contribute to the readability and impact of the document.	
2.6	Deliver multimedia presentations: **a.** Combine text, images, and sound and draw information from many sources (e.g., television broadcasts, videos, films, newspapers, magazines, CD-ROMs, the Internet, electronic media-generated images). **b.** Select an appropriate medium for each element of the presentation. **c.** Use the selected media skillfully, editing appropriately and monitoring for quality. **d.** Test the audience's response and revise the presentation accordingly.	144-148

Writing and Speaking Resources

Written and Oral English Language Conventions

1.0	Students write and speak with a command of standard English conventions.	48, 49, 62, 63, 76, 77, 90, 91, 105, 106, 118, 119
1.1	Demonstrate control of grammar, diction, and paragraph and sentence structure and an understanding of English usage.	48, 49, 62, 76, 90, 91, 105, 106, 118, 119
1.2	Produce legible work that shows accurate spelling and correct punctuation and capitalization.	48, 49, 62, 63, 76, 77, 90, 91, 105, 106, 118, 119
1.3	Reflect appropriate manuscript requirements in writing.	49, 63, 77, 90, 105, 119

Listening and Speaking

1.0	Students formulate adroit judgments about oral communication. They deliver focused and coherent presentations that convey clear and distinct perspectives and demonstrate solid reasoning. They use gestures, tone, and vocabulary tailored to the audience and purpose.	123–148
1.1	Recognize strategies used by the media to inform, persuade, entertain, and transmit culture (e.g., advertisements; perpetuation of stereotypes; use of visual representations, special effects, language).	144–148
1.2	Analyze the impact of the media on the democratic process (e.g., exerting influence on elections, creating images of leaders, shaping attitudes) at the local, state, and national levels.	144–148
1.3	Interpret and evaluate the various ways in which events are presented and information is communicated by visual image makers (e.g., graphic artists, documentary filmmakers, illustrators, news photographers).	144–148
1.4	Use rhetorical questions, parallel structure, concrete images, figurative language, characterization, irony, and dialogue to achieve clarity, force, and aesthetic effect.	127–131, 140–143
1.5	Distinguish between and use various forms of classical and contemporary logical arguments, including: a. Inductive and deductive reasoning b. Syllogisms and analogies	123–126
1.6	Use logical, ethical, and emotional appeals that enhance a specific tone and purpose.	123–126
1.7	Use appropriate rehearsal strategies to pay attention to performance details, achieve command of the text, and create skillful artistic staging.	123-126, 127–131, 132–135, 136-139, 140–143
1.8	Use effective and interesting language, including: a. Informal expressions for effect b. Standard American English for clarity c. Technical language for specificity	132–135, 136–139
1.9	Use research and analysis to justify strategies for gesture, movement, and vocalization, including dialect, pronunciation, and enunciation.	123–126, 132–135, 136–139, 140–143
1.10	Evaluate when to use different kinds of effects (e.g., visual, music, sound, graphics) to create effective productions.	132–135, 136–139, 140–143
1.11	Critique a speaker's diction and syntax in relation to the purpose of an oral communication and the impact the words may have on the audience.	144–148

Writing and Speaking Resources

1.12	Identify logical fallacies used in oral addresses (e.g., attack ad hominem, false causality, red herring, overgeneralization, bandwagon effect).	123–126, 144–148
1.13	Analyze the four basic types of persuasive speech (i.e., propositions of fact, value, problem, or policy) and understand the similarities and differences in their patterns of organization and the use of persuasive language, reasoning, and proof.	144–148
1.14	Analyze the techniques used in media messages for a particular audience and evaluate their effectiveness (e.g., Orson Welles' radio broadcast "War of the Worlds").	144–148
2.0	Students deliver polished formal and extemporaneous presentations that combine traditional rhetorical strategies of narration, exposition, persuasion, and description. Student speaking demonstrates a command of standard American English and the organizational and delivery strategies outlined in Listening and Speaking Standard 1.0.	123–143
2.1	Deliver reflective presentations: a. Explore the significance of personal experiences, events, conditions, or concerns, using appropriate rhetorical strategies (e.g., narration, description, exposition, persuasion). b. Draw comparisons between the specific incident and broader themes that illustrate the speaker's beliefs or generalizations about life. c. Maintain a balance between describing the incident and relating it to more general, abstract ideas.	136–139
2.2	Deliver oral reports on historical investigations: a. Use exposition, narration, description, persuasion, or some combination of those to support the thesis. b. Analyze several historical records of a single event, examining critical relationships between elements of the research topic. c. Explain the perceived reason or reasons for the similarities and differences by using information derived from primary and secondary sources to support or enhance the presentation. d. Include information on all relevant perspectives and consider the validity and reliability of sources.	132–135
2.3	Deliver oral responses to literature: a. Demonstrate a comprehensive understanding of the significant ideas of literary works (e.g., make assertions about the text that are reasonable and supportable). b. Analyze the imagery, language, universal themes, and unique aspects of the text through the use of rhetorical strategies (e.g., narration, description, persuasion, exposition, a combination of those strategies). c. Support important ideas and viewpoints through accurate and detailed references to the text or to other works. d. Demonstrate an awareness of the author's use of stylistic devices and an appreciation of the effects created. e. Identify and assess the impact of perceived ambiguities, nuances, and complexities within the text.	140–143
2.4	Deliver multimedia presentations: a. Combine text, images, and sound by incorporating information from a wide range of media, including films, newspapers, magazines, CD-ROMs, online information, television, videos, and electronic media-generated images. b. Select an appropriate medium for each element of the presentation. c. Use the selected media skillfully, editing appropriately and monitoring for quality. d. Test the audience's response and revise the presentation accordingly.	140–143, 144–148
2.5	Recite poems, selections from speeches, or dramatic soliloquies with attention to performance details to achieve clarity, force, and aesthetic effect and to demonstrate an understanding of the meaning (e.g., Hamlet's soliloquy "To Be or Not to Be").	127–131

Writing and Speaking Resources

Academic Vocabulary

Academic vocabulary refers to the vocabulary you need to know when you discuss subjects taught in school. Each subject has its own academic vocabulary. Below are terms that will help you discuss the writing and speaking projects in this book.

Analysis The study of how individual parts of a subject make up its whole.

Audience A group of listeners, spectators, or readers.

Bias A viewpoint in favor of or against an issue, with a tendency to be strongly one-sided.

Character An individual in a story, play, or other literary work.

Conflict A struggle or clash between opposing characters or opposing forces.

Consequences Thoughts, feelings, behaviors, or events that are caused by a previous thought, feeling, behavior, or event.

Evidence The support or proof that backs up an idea, conclusion, or opinion. Evidence can be in the form of examples, quotations from experts, statistics, and personal experiences.

Figurative Language Language that describes one thing in terms of something else and is not literally true. Figures of speech always involve some sort of imaginative comparison between seemingly unlike things.

- **Simile** A comparison between two unlike things using a word such as *like, as, than,* or *resembles.*

- **Metaphor** A comparison between two unlike things in which one thing becomes another thing.

- **Personification** A special kind of metaphor in which a nonhuman or nonliving thing or quality is talked about as if it were human or alive.

Generalization A generalization is a broad statement based on several particular situations.

Imagery The use of language to evoke a picture or a concrete sensation of a person, a thing, a place, or an experience.

Interpretation An explanation of the meaning of an author's work. Interpretations vary among individuals.

Main Idea The most important idea expressed in a piece of writing. Sometimes the main idea is stated directly by the writer; at other times the reader must infer it.

Message The theme, main idea, or lesson in a piece of writing or a speech. What the author or speaker wants the audience to know.

Nonverbal Signals Types of body language that communicate without the use of words.

- **Eye Contact** A contact that occurs when two people look directly at each other.

- **Facial Expression** A communication involving movements of the face that conveys a feeling or a mood; for example, a smile, frown, or raised eyebrow.

- **Gesture** A type of body movement that conveys a nonverbal message, or an act performed to show feelings.

- **Posture** The position of the body, sometimes intentionally assumed in order to communicate an attitude or feeling.

Paraphrase A restatement of the ideas and information in a written work.

Plagiarism Taking words or ideas from an existing source without crediting that source, and passing them off as one's own.

Plot The series of related events that make up a story.

Point of View The vantage point from which a story is told. Also see *bias* for nonfiction texts.

- **First person** The first-person point of view in which one of the characters, using the personal pronoun *I*, is telling the story.

- **Omniscient** The all-knowing, third person point of view in which the narrator knows everything about the characters.

- **Third-person limited** The narrator, who plays no part in the story, zooms in on the thoughts and feelings of one character.

Propaganda An organized attempt to influence a large audience of readers, listeners, or TV watchers.

- **Bandwagon** An appeal that urges you to do or believe something just because everyone else does.
- **Testimonial** An appeal that uses a famous person to testify that he or she supports the issue or uses the product.
- **Snob Appeal** The suggestion that by using this product you can be superior to others.
- **Stereotyping** Referring to members of a group as if they were all the same.

Purpose The reason why a person writes or speaks, formally or informally. The purpose may be to inform, to persuade, to express feelings, or to entertain.

Research To closely investigate and gather information on a topic in order to establish facts.

Rhetorical Devices Using language in a story or speech to achieve a particular effect or to cause an emotional response from the audience.

- **Cadence** The flow or rhythm of a series of words in a pattern that varies and is without structure.
- **Repetition** A literary device in which the writer purposely repeats words and sentences within a work.
- **Onomatopoeia** The use of a word whose sound imitates or suggests its meaning. *Boom, bang, sniffle, rumble, hush, ding, and snort* are all examples of onomatopoeia.

Setting The time and place of a story.

Source The original location where ideas and information are found, such as a reference book or Web page.

Speaking Techniques Methods that a speaker uses to "grab" and maintain an audience's attention.

- **Voice Modulation** A technique in which the volume, pitch, or tone of a speaker's voice is varied to engage an audience and keep its attention.
- **Inflection** A technique in which the speaker makes his or her voice louder or softer to emphasize certain words or phrases.
- **Tempo** A technique in which the speaker varies the speed of his or her speech.
- **Enunciation** A technique in which words are carefully and precisely pronounced.
- **Eye Contact** A technique that involves the speaker directing his or her gaze into the eyes of audience members.
- **Verbal Signals** Using one's voice to convey the overall feeling or emotion of an oral communication.
- **Pitch** The high or low sounds of one's voice.
- **Tone** The attitude a writer or speaker takes toward his or her subject or audience.
- **Diction** A speaker's choice of words and the way in which they are organized.

Style The distinctive way in which a writer uses language.

Summarizing Restating the author's main points in your own words.

Suspense The anxious curiosity the reader feels about what will happen next in a story.

Theme The insight about human life that is revealed in literary work.

Topic The issue or subject to be addressed.

Validity Being true or strongly believable based on well-grounded, logical, and justifiable evidence.

Voice A writer's unique expression of himself or herself.

Writing Prompt A suggestion of a scenario designed to help a writer pick a topic aimed at a specific type of writing.

Why It Matters

We humans have the unique ability to use words and images to communicate. From our infant babbling and gesturing, we develop our communication skills to accomplish increasingly complex and sophisticated purposes. Through observation and formal study, we learn to communicate one way within our families, perhaps another way with our peers, and still other ways in school, at work, and in society. We learn to vary our word choices and grammatical constructions according to our audience and purpose.

But no matter whether we express our messages informally or formally, on the spur of the moment or after careful thought, their content falls into one or more of four basic types: *narrative, expository, descriptive,* and *persuasive.* The type of writing or speech you choose for a specific situation will depend on whether your purpose for communicating is to *inform* or *explain,* to *express* or *entertain,* or to *influence or persuade.*

NARRATIVE WRITING AND SPEAKING

Narrative writing and speaking uses **chronological order** to tell a story or relate a sequence of events. Narratives are used both to entertain and to enlighten readers and listeners. You might write a funny or suspenseful fictional story to entertain your friends or write a serious real-life narrative to tell others about a time in your life that has helped shape the person you are today. You also use narrative skills to tell others about the traffic accident you witnessed or the soccer game you watched. In the business world, you might use narrative writing in your report on an inspection visit you made to a particular facility or to document a problem with a process.

You encounter narrative writing and speaking whenever you see, hear, or read material such as the following:

- TV sitcoms
- Documentaries
- News reports
- History books
- Short stories and novels
- Tell-all Hollywood gossip
- Breakup songs
- Comic books
- Action/adventure video games

EXPOSITORY WRITING AND SPEAKING

Expository writing and speaking seeks to explain and inform. Expository communication may explain how to do something or how something works. It may also explain facts or ideas. Because explanations are clarified by organizing information into categories, exposition frequently uses **logical order.** Explanations also frequently contain factual and statistical information. In business, you will use expository writing in various types of analytical reports.

You encounter expository writing and speaking whenever you see, hear, or read material such as the following:

- Academic lectures
- Science books
- Product labels
- Meeting minutes
- Encyclopedia articles
- Press releases
- Recipes
- Repair manuals
- Computer-program help screens

Writing and Speaking Resources

DESCRIPTIVE WRITING AND SPEAKING

Descriptive writing and speaking helps the audience "see" a clear picture of a person, an object, or a scene. Descriptions are often presented in a **spatial order** and usually contain **sensory details**—specific nouns and verbs as well as vivid adjectives and adverbs that appeal to the senses. Rather than explicitly stating a main idea in a topic sentence, descriptive paragraphs may rely on details to provide clues to an implied main idea, sometimes referred to as a dominant impression. Descriptions may emphasize factual details or try to evoke an emotional response from the readers or listeners. You might factually describe an item for a "For Sale" advertisement, or you may want to go beyond a brief postcard and write your friend an engaging description of your vacation spot. When your grandfather reminisces about his boyhood on the farm, you may want to record some of his memories for a family history book.

You encounter descriptive writing and speaking whenever you see, hear, or read material such as the following:

- Travel brochures
- Product catalogs
- Job descriptions
- Lost and found listings
- Technical manuals
- Biographies
- Restaurant menus
- Diary entries
- Play-by-play radio sportscasters

PERSUASIVE WRITING AND SPEAKING

Persuasive writing and speaking expresses one's opinion or issues a call to action. Such communications are usually arranged by **order of importance** or **logical order.** Persuasive essays, editorials, advertisements, and speeches examine issues and attempt to influence the opinions, beliefs, or actions of the reader, viewer, or listener. Perhaps you want to write a letter to the student council recommending that more students get involved in a certain service project. You might petition a legislature asking that they take a particular stand on an issue of concern.

If your career path takes you into the worlds of marketing, advertising, courtroom law, politics, or even counseling and social service, you will obviously need persuasive skills. But even the most technical scientist may need to employ persuasion in a request for funding, while an entry-level clerk might write a persuasive memo for the office suggestion box.

You encounter persuasive writing and speaking whenever you see, hear, or read material such as the following:

- Petitions
- Proposals
- Sales pitches
- Political campaign speeches
- Business correspondence
- Resumes and cover letters
- Newspaper editorials
- TV commercials
- Political demonstrations

Writing and Speaking Resources

Your Writing Process

PREWRITING

- Choose a **form** and a manageable **topic.**
- Identify your **purpose and audience.**
- Draft a sentence that expresses your **main idea.**
- **Gather information** about the topic.
- Begin to **organize** the information.

WRITING

- Draft an **introduction** that gets your reader's attention and states your main idea.
- Provide **background information.**
- Follow a **plan** for organizing your ideas.
- State your **supporting points** and **elaborate** on them.
- Wrap things up with a **conclusion.**

REVISING

- **Evaluate** your draft, or ask a peer to evaluate it.
- **Revise the draft** to improve its content, organization, and style.

PUBLISHING

- **Proofread** your draft to find and correct spelling, punctuation, and grammar errors.
- **Use** correct manuscript style.
- **Publish** your writing.
- **Reflect** on your writing experience.

Writing and Speaking Resources

Think Sheets and Summaries

HOW TO CREATE A THINK SHEET

1. Write the title and author of the selection at the top of a sheet of notebook paper. Then, draw a vertical line down the center of the sheet. Label the left-hand column "text" and the right-hand column "responses."

2. As you read the selection, in the left-hand column of your paper, note words or brief passages that catch your interest or seem important.

3. Next to each word or passage noted on your paper, jot down the response in the right-hand column. Include notes on any of the following:
   - use of language
   - organization of information, such as comparison-contrast structure
   - strategies for developing ideas and elaborating, such as using anecdotes or descriptions

4. When you have finished reading, add to your response column any related ideas or answers you have found to earlier questions.

HOW TO CREATE A SUMMARY

1. First, read the selection carefully.

2. Then, skim the selection looking for sections. Sometimes, each section begins with a heading. If a selection has no headings, consider each paragraph a section. On a sheet of paper, list a phrase identifying the general topic of each section.

3. Under each phrase listed on your paper, write in your own words a sentence identifying the most important ideas included in that section. Make note of the section's main idea and most important supporting points, or details. These will be the points, or details, for which the writer provides the most elaboration.

4. Combine your section summaries into a paragraph, using transitions to link the ideas.

Writing and Speaking Resources

Building Coherence

TYPES OF ORDER

Order	When to Use	How It Works
Chronological	• to tell a story • to explain a process	• presents actions and events according to the order in which they occur
Spatial	• to describe a place or an object	• arranges details according to their location in space
Logical	• to explain or classify (by defining, dividing, or comparing and contrasting)	• groups related ideas together to show their relationship
Order of Importance	• to inform or to persuade	• arranges details from most important to least important, or vice versa

CONNECTING IDEAS

Connecting Strategy	How It Works
Direct References	• use a noun or pronoun that refers to a noun or pronoun used earlier • repeat a word used earlier • use a word or phrase that means the same thing as one used earlier
Transitional Expressions (including prepositions that show chronological or spatial order)	• compare ideas (*also, and, besides, in addition, similarly, too*) • contrast ideas (*although, but, however, instead, nevertheless, otherwise, yet*) • show cause and effect (*as a result, because, consequently, so, therefore, thus*) • show time (*after, before, eventually, finally, first, meanwhile, then, when*) • show place (*above, across, around, beyond, from, here, in, on, over, there, to, under*) • show importance (*first, last, mainly, then, to begin with*)

Writing and Speaking Resources

Strategies for Evaluating and Revising

EVALUATE YOUR DRAFT

Re-read.	Re-read your draft carefully—not once, but several times—focusing on content, organization, and style.
Ask.	Ask a peer to read the draft, point out weak or confusing parts, and make suggestions.

REVISE CONTENT AND ORGANIZATION

Add.	Add sensory or factual details, examples, and illustrations. Add sentences and paragraphs. Add words and phrases (such as, *as a result, for example, first, and however*) to connect ideas.
Delete.	Delete words, sentences, and paragraphs that stray from your composition's main idea. Eliminate wordiness and unnecessary repetition.
Replace.	Replace weak support with stronger points, more convincing logical evidence, or details that are more vivid.
Rearrange.	Rearrange sentences and paragraphs to find the clearest order of ideas. Use the cut-and-paste function of a word-processing program to experiment with various arrangements.
Elaborate.	Elaborate and support each main point by providing specific details, facts, examples, illustrations, sensory images, figurative details, quotations, or anecdotes.

REVISE STYLE

Fine-tune.	Check to make sure each word you have used is the one that most precisely communicates your idea.
Eliminate.	Eliminate clichés and slang.
Vary.	Vary sentence length and structure. Combine sentences to add variety or complexity.
Avoid.	Avoid using the passive voice.

Writing and Speaking Resources

Student Self-Evaluation Rubrics for the Six Traits

Use these rubrics to evaluate your writing. Be honest! If your paper is strong, you will be able to answer "yes" to the first set of questions. If your answers are "no," use the other two sets of questions to identify where your paper needs more work.

SIX TRAITS RUBRIC: IDEAS AND CONTENT

5 It's Crystal Clear!

- Is my topic clearly focused—neither too broad nor too narrow—for a paper of its kind?
- Are my ideas original, interesting, and creative?
- Do I draw from personal experience or knowledge?
- Are my details insightful and well chosen? Or are they obvious, predictable, or clichéd—not good?
- Is my development of the topic thorough and logical? Have I anticipated and answered the reader's questions?
- Are my supporting details accurate and relevant? Does every detail contribute to the whole?

3 Close—My Ideas Need a Little Polishing

- Could I develop my topic a little better? Do I make my readers work to figure out my purpose and predict how my ideas will develop?
- Are my supporting details present but maybe too vague? Could they illustrate the main idea or theme better?
- Do I refer to my own experience or knowledge but maybe fail to push beyond the obvious to more specific ideas?
- Are my ideas understandable but maybe not detailed, elaborated upon, or personalized? Do I need to work more on understanding my topic or task?
- Do I stray from the topic? Are my ideas too general? Do I force readers to rely on what they already know to make sense of the paper?

1 Hmm. What Am I Trying to Say?

- Have I forgotten to decide on a topic or main idea? Does my paper read like a rough draft or brainstorming notes?
- Is my thesis a vague statement about the topic or a restatement of a prompt? Does it need more support, detail, or insight?
- Do I need to add information or give my readers clearer connections?
- Is my text rambling and repetitious? Are my ideas not developed enough? Is the paper too short?
- Does every idea and detail in my paper seem equally weighted? Do my ideas add up to a main idea, thesis, or theme?

Writing and Speaking Resources

SIX TRAITS RUBRIC: ORGANIZATION

5 Yes! I Can See Where This Is Going!

- Does my paper use a logical and effective sequence of ideas?
- Does the paper contain both an attention-grabbing introduction and a satisfying conclusion?
- Is my pacing carefully controlled? Do I slow down to provide explanation or elaboration when appropriate and increase the pace when necessary?
- Do my transitions make clear connections and cue the reader to specific relationships between ideas?
- Is my organizational structure appropriate to my purpose and audience?
- If present, does my title sum up the central idea of the paper in a fresh way?

3 Close—Wait, I Think I Need More Structure

- Does my paper have both an introduction and a conclusion? Are they as engaging and coherent as they can be?
- Is my sequence logical but predictable? Could it be more compelling?
- Does my sequence fail to consistently support my paper's ideas? Do I make my readers reorder sections mentally or provide transitions as they read?
- Is my pacing reasonably well done? Do I move ahead too quickly or linger over unimportant ideas?
- Are the transitions between ideas clear enough?
- If present, is my title maybe a little dull or lacking insight?

1 Hmm. Even *I'm* a Little Lost

- Is the sequence in my paper broken—maybe each idea or event does not logically follow the previous one? Does my paper lack organizational structure, such as clear paragraph breaks?
- Does my paper lack a clear introduction to guide readers and a conclusion that sums up ideas at the end?
- Is my pacing halting or inconsistent? Do I know when to slow down or speed up the pace in order to help my readers understand?
- Are the transitions between my ideas confusing or absent?
- If present, does my title accurately reflect the content of the paper? If not, why not?

Writing and Speaking Resources

SIX TRAITS RUBRIC: VOICE

5 Yes! I Can Really Hear My Own Voice

- Is the tone of my writing appropriate for the paper's purpose and audience?
- Do I reveal myself as a real person behind the text? Do I take risks in revealing my personality throughout the piece?
- If my paper is expository or persuasive, do I show a strong connection to the topic and explain why readers should care about the issue?
- If my paper is narrative, is my point of view sincere, interesting, and compelling?

3 Close. I Need to Try Again With Feeling

- Do I offer only generalities instead of personal insights? Does my writing feel impersonal?
- Do I use neutral language and a flat tone instead of an interested lively one?
- Do I communicate in an earnest and pleasing manner but forget to take risks? Do I need to inspire or engage my reader more?
- Do I really share my own interest in the topic with my audience? Do I need to build more credibility with the audience?
- Does my narrative fail to reveal a fresh or individual perspective?

1 Hmm. I Can Barely Hear Myself Speaking

- Is it true that I don't really think about the audience—that I use a voice that may not be appropriate for the intended reader?
- Is the development of my topic too limited, so that no clear point of view is present? Is my writing so short that readers don't get to know me?
- Do I seem to speak in a monotone, using a voice that lacks excitement about the message or topic?
- Does my expository or persuasive writing lack accurate information or use overly technical language? Does my narrative writing lack a point of view and fail to inspire interest?

SIX TRAITS RUBRIC: WORD CHOICE

5 Yes! My Words Come Through Loud and Clear
• Are all my words specific and appropriate? In all instances, have I taken care to choose the right words or phrases?
• Is my paper's language controlled and natural, not overdone? Do I rarely use clichés and jargon?
• Does my paper contain energetic verbs, precise nouns, and clear modifiers?
• Do I use vivid words and phrases, including sensory details to create distinct images in the reader's mind?
3 Close—With a Little Polish My Words Will Shine
• Are my words correct and generally adequate but maybe lacking in originality or precision?
• Do I use familiar words and phrases that do not grab the reader's interest or imagination or only occasionally use lively verbs and phrases to perk things up?
• Do my attempts at using engaging or academic language seem overly showy?
• Does my writing contain passive verbs and basic nouns? Does it lack clarifying adjectives and precise adverbs?
1 Hmm. Even I Don't Understand What I Mean
• Does my language lack precision? Does my vague language make the reader feel confused and unsure of my purpose?
• Have I made some inaccurate word choices? Are some of my words used as the wrong part of speech?
• Do I repeat myself or use certain words too much?
• Have I used unexplained jargon or clichés?

SIX TRAITS RUBRIC: SENTENCE FLUENCY

5 Yes! My Sentences Really Flow
• Have I constructed sentences so that my meaning is clear to the reader?
• Do my sentences vary in length and in structure?
• Do I use varied sentence beginnings to add interest and clarity?
• Does my writing have a steady rhythm? Is my reader able to read the text effortlessly without confusion or stumbling?
• Is my use of dialogue natural? Do I use sentence fragments thoughtfully?
• Do I use clear connectives and transitions between sentences to reveal how the paper's ideas work together?

3 Close—I Feel Like I'm Drifting Off Course
• Are my sentences usually grammatical and unified but dull? Have I forgotten to pay enough attention to how the sentences sound?
• Is there some variation in sentence length and structure as well as in sentence beginnings or are all of my sentences constructed exactly the same way?
• Do I make my reader search for transitional words and phrases that show how sentences relate to one another? Do I forget to use context clues?
• Even though I have written expressively, are there passages with stilted or awkward sentences?

1 Hmm. I'm a Little Lost
• Do my sentences just not "hang together"? Have I used run-on, incomplete, monotonous, or awkward sentences?
• Does my phrasing often sound too singsong? Is my paper kind of dull to read aloud?
• Do most of my sentences begin the same way and follow the same pattern (e.g., subject-verb-object)?
• Have I used too many connectives or too few—so that my writing sometimes sounds confused?

Writing and Speaking Resources

SIX TRAITS RUBRIC: CONVENTIONS

5 Yes! It's Nearly Perfect!

- Is my paragraphing regular? Does it enhance the organization of the paper?
- Are my grammar and usage correct? Do they add clarity and style to the text?
- Is my punctuation accurate and does it enable the reader to move through the text with understanding and ease?
- Is my understanding of capitalization rules evident throughout the paper?
- Are most words, even difficult ones, spelled correctly?
- Is what I've written long and complex enough to show that I understand a wide range of convention skills?

3 Close—I Found a Few Errors

- Do I run together ideas that should be in separate paragraphs? Do I start paragraphs in the middle of an idea?
- Does my writing have a few grammar and usage errors—but not enough to confuse my readers?
- Are my end marks usually in the correct place but other punctuation marks (such as commas, apostrophes, semi-colons, and parentheses) perhaps missing or used incorrectly?
- Have I spelled common words correctly for the most part?
- Are most words capitalized correctly or is my command of capitalization skills a little shaky?

1 Hmm. I'm Distracted By Too Many Errors

- Am I missing formal paragraphs? Do my paragraphs "forget" to support my content or organization?
- Have I made a lot of errors in grammar and usage? Do my errors distract or confuse the reader?
- Is my punctuation, including end marks, often missing or incorrect?
- Have I misspelled common words?
- Have I consistently made errors in capitalization?
- Does my paper need to be read once just to decode the language and then again to understand my meaning?

ONE MORE TRAIT: PRESENTATION/PUBLICATION

5 Yes! My Paper Is Clear and Pleasing to the Eye

- If my paper is handwritten, is the slant of my writing consistent and the spacing between my words uniform?
- If my paper is word-processed, have I used appropriate fonts and font sizes?
- Have I used enough white space (margins, spacing) so that my paper is easy to read?
- If I have included a title, headings and subheadings, bullets, and page numbering, are they consistent and do they make the paper easy to read?
- If I have used visuals—graphs, tables, maps, or other graphics—in my paper, are they clear and placed logically?

3 Close—My Paper Is a Little Cluttered

- Is my handwriting readable but maybe a little sloppy or inconsistent?
- Have I used too many fonts or is my chosen font or font size hard to read?
- Have I used just enough white space? Or are my margins too wide or too narrow? Is the space between paragraphs too much or too little?
- When I use titles, headings and subheadings, bullets, and page numbering, are they used inconsistently or do they get in the way of the reading?
- Have I placed visuals—graphs, tables, maps, or other graphics—in the wrong places or too far from the text they help explain? Do they take up too much space or they too small to read?

1 Hmm. I'm Distracted By the Way the Page Looks

- Has poor handwriting made my paper too difficult to read?
- Has my use of interesting fonts or too many fonts and font sizes made my paper difficult to read?
- Is my use of white space (margins, spacing) too random or confusing for readers to see and read the text?
- Does my paper need a title, headings and subheadings, bullets, or page numbers that would help a reader navigate through the paper?
- Have I used visuals—graphs, tables, maps, or other graphics—that mislead or confuse my readers? Are my visuals appropriate or too technical? Should I leave them out or find new ones?

Proofreading Guidelines and Symbols

GUIDELINES FOR PROOFREADING	Yes	No	Needs Work
Is every sentence complete, not a fragment or a run-on?			
Are punctuation marks—such as end marks, commas, semicolons, colons, dashes, and quotation marks—used correctly?			
Are proper nouns, proper adjectives, and the first words of sentences capitalized?			
Does every verb agree in number with its subject?			
Are verbs and tenses used correctly?			
Are subject and object forms of personal pronouns used correctly?			
Does every pronoun agree with its antecedent in number and in gender? Are pronoun references clear?			
Are frequently confused words (such as *fewer* and *less, affect* and *effect)* used correctly?			
Are all words spelled correctly? Are the plural forms of words correct?			
Is the paper neat and correct in form?			

Writing and Speaking Resources

	Symbols for Editing and Proofreading	
Symbol	**Example**	**Meaning of Symbol**
≡	Fifty-first <u>street</u>	Capitalize a lowercase letter.
/	Jerry's Aunt	Lowercase a capital letter.
∧	differ^eant	Change a letter.
∧	the capital ^of Ohio	Insert a missing word, letter or punctuation mark.
⌒	beside the ~~river~~ lake	Replace a word.
ℐ	Where's the ~~the~~ key?	Leave out a word, letter, or punctuation mark.
⊥	an invisible guest	Leave out and close up.
⌢	a close friend ship	Close up space.
∪	thier	Change the order of letters.
(tr)	Avoid having too many corrections of your paper in the final version.	Transpose the circled words. Write *tr* in nearby margin.
⁋	⁋"Hi," he smiled.	Begin a new paragraph.
⊙	Stay well	Add a period.
∧	Of course you may be wrong.	Add a comma.
#	ice#hockey	Add a space.
⨀	one of the following	Add a colon.
∧;	Maria Simmons, M.D. Jim Fiorello, Ph.D.	Add a semicolon.
=	a well=known writer	Add a hyphen.
∨	Pauls car	Add an apostrophe.
(stet)	On the fifteenth of ~~July~~	Keep the crossed-out material. (Write stet in nearby margin.)

Active-Listening Strategies

BE AN ACTIVE LISTENER

- **Make frequent eye contact with the speaker.** Looking at the speaker will help you stay interested. It also encourages the speaker.

- **Ask yourself questions as you listen.** Questioning yourself can help you understand better.

- **Relate what you are hearing to what you already know.** Connecting new knowledge with what you already know helps you remember what you hear.

- **Take notes.** Use abbreviations to write key points. Note questions you can ask to clarify a point or to further your understanding.

AVOID DISTRACTIONS

- **If you are easily distracted, consider sitting near the front of the room.** It is easy to get distracted when you sit toward the back. You may also not be able to see visuals or hear the speaker as well.

- **Focus on the speaker.** Try to ignore any distractions around you.

- **Don't get distracted by visuals.** Good visuals help the speaker make a point. Sometimes, poor visuals can actually distract you from the speech. Don't let visuals distract you from the point of the speech.

RESPOND APPROPRIATELY

- **When asking a question, refer to information you have heard.** This way, speakers will know what information you need to have clarified and will know that you have been listening.

- **Ask questions after the speaker is finished.** Use questions to help you better understand what has been said.

- **Restate what is heard.** Summarize in your own words to make sure you understand.

- **Use only constructive criticism.** When evaluating your peers, provide them with only helpful suggestions. Always be polite. Think of at least one positive comment.

- **Respond to criticism politely.** Listen to what your peers have to say, and note their suggestions for improvement. Do not get overly defensive if you disagree with someone evaluating your work.

Writing and Speaking Resources

Effective Speaking Strategies

USE VERBAL TECHNIQUES

- **Speak at an appropriate rate.** Your rate is how quickly you speak. Nervous speakers often speak too quickly. If you have difficulty slowing down, try taking frequent pauses instead.

- **Use an appropriate volume.** Your volume is how loudly you speak. Adjust your volume so everyone can hear you. Vary your volume to create an effect. For example, when telling a story, speak softly to express shyness.

- **Vary the pitch of your voice.** The pitch is the highness or lowness of your voice. Don't speak in a monotone. Vary the pitch of your voice to keep your audience interested and to emphasize important words.

- **Adjust the tone of your voice.** Your tone is the attitude you express. Match the tone of your voice to your message.

- **Enunciate your words.** Enunciating is pronouncing words clearly. Speak carefully so your audience can understand you.

- **Use pauses effectively.** Pauses can emphasize key words or ideas.

- **Stress key words you want your audience to remember.** You can stress words by pausing before saying them, by saying them slightly louder, or by using a different pitch when saying them.

USE NONVERBAL TECHNIQUES

- **Make frequent eye contact.** Look at your audience to show you are confident. Be sure to look at people in different parts of the room.

- **Use appropriate gestures.** Gestures are movements you make with your body, such as nodding or pointing. Use them to stress a particular point. Your gestures should be relaxed and varied. Be careful, however, not to use too many gestures. Doing so can be distracting.

- **Use facial expressions.** Use facial expressions, such as smiling or frowning, to show your feelings and to emphasize parts of your message.

- **Maintain good posture.** Stand straight with both feet on the floor and with your arms relaxed at your sides. Good posture will make you appear confident.

Writing and Speaking Resources

My Writing and Speaking Records

My Writing and Speaking Records

Writing Record

Ratings: ✓✓✓✓ One of my best!   ✓✓ OK, but not my best

✓✓✓ Better if I revise it   ✓ I don't like this one.

Month/Day	Title and type of writing	Notes about this piece of writing	Rating

Spelling Log

Word	My misspelling	How to remember correct spelling

Goal-Setting for Writing

GOAL	STEPS TO REACH GOAL	REVIEW OF PROGRESS
Writing Goals		

Goal-Setting for Listening and Speaking

GOAL	STEPS TO REACH GOAL	REVIEW OF PROGRESS
Listening Goals		
Speaking Goals		

Summary of Progress: Writing, Listening, and Speaking

Complete this form before sitting down with your teacher or a classmate to assess your overall progress, set goals, or discuss specific pieces of your work.

Grade: _____   School year: _____   Date of summary: _____

What work have I done so far this year?	What project do I plan to work on next?
Writing: Listening: Speaking:	Writing: Listening: Speaking:
What do I think of my progress? What about my work has improved? What needs to be better?	**Which examples of my work are my favorites and why?**

Summary of Progress, *continued*

Which pieces of my work need more revision, and what is needed?	How has listening or speaking helped me in preparing for papers or other projects this year?

What a classmate or the teacher thinks about my progress

In writing—

In listening—

In speaking—

Writing Self-Inventory

Questions and answers about my writing	More about my answers
How often do I write?	What types of writing do I do?
Where, besides school, do I write?	What kind of writing do I do there?
Do I like to write?	Why or why not?
Of the things I have written, I like these best:	Why do I like them best?
What topics do I like to write about?	Why do I like to write about these topics?
Is anything about writing difficult for me? What?	Why do I think it is difficult?
Does reading help me to be a better writer or vice versa?	Why do I think this?
How important is learning to write well?	Why do I think this?

Writing Process Self-Evaluation

Use the chart below to analyze your writing process. Circle the numbers that most clearly indicate how well you meet the stated criteria in your writing process. The lowest possible total score is 5, the highest, 20.

1 = Do not meet these criteria

2 = Attempt to meet these criteria but need to improve

3 = Fairly successful in meeting criteria

4 = Clearly meet these criteria

Title of paper _____

Stage in Writing Process	Criteria for Evaluation	Rating
Prewriting	• Use prewriting techniques to find and limit subject and to gather details about subject • Organize details in a reasonable way	1 2 3 4
Writing	• Get most of ideas down on paper in a rough draft	1 2 3 4
Revising	• Do complete peer- or self-evaluation • Find ways to improve content, organization, and style of rough draft • Revise by adding, cutting, replacing, and moving material	1 2 3 4
Proofreading	• Correct errors in spelling, grammar, usage, punctuation, capitalization, and manuscript form	1 2 3 4
Publishing and Reflecting	• Produce a clean final copy in proper form • Share the piece of writing with others • Reflect on the writing process and on the paper's strengths and weaknesses	1 2 3 4

Additional Comments:

_____

_____

_____

_____

_____

Proofreading Strategies

Proofread your paper using one of the following steps. Put a check by the step you used.

_____ 1. Read the paper backward word by word.

_____ 2. Make a large card with a one- or two-inch-sized strip cut into it and read every word in the paper one at a time, through the hole.

_____ 3. Read the first sentence in your paper carefully. Put your left index finger on the punctuation mark that signals the end of that sentence. Now, put your right index finger on the punctuation mark that ends the second sentence. Carefully read the material between your fingers; then, move your left index finger to the end of the second sentence and your right to the end of the third sentence, and read carefully. Keep moving your fingers until you have carefully examined each sentence in the paper.

List the mistakes you discovered when proofreading.

_____

_____

_____

_____

_____

_____

_____

_____

_____

_____

_____

_____

_____

_____

Proofreading Checklist

**Read through the paper and then mark the following statements either *T* for true
or *F* for false.**

Writer's name _____   **Title of paper** _____

_____   1. The paper is neat.

_____   2. Each sentence begins with a capital letter.

_____   3. Each sentence ends with a period, question mark, or exclamation mark.

_____   4. Each sentence is complete. Each has a subject and a predicate and expresses a complete
thought.

_____   5. Run-on sentences are avoided.

_____   6. A singular verb is used with each singular subject and a plural verb with each plural
subject.

_____   7. Nominative case pronouns such as *I* and *we* are used for subjects; objective case
pronouns such as *me* and *us* are used for objects.

_____   8. Singular pronouns are used to refer to singular nouns, and plural pronouns are used to
refer to plural nouns.

_____   9. Indefinite pronoun references are avoided.

_____ 10. Each word is spelled correctly.

_____ 11. Frequently confused words, such as *lie/lay, sit/set, rise/raise, all ready/already,* and
fewer/less, are used correctly.

_____ 12. Double negatives are avoided.

_____ 13. All proper nouns and proper adjectives are capitalized.

_____ 14. Word endings such as *–s, –ing,* and *–ed* are included where they should be.

_____ 15. No words have been accidentally left out or accidentally written twice.

_____ 16. Each paragraph is indented.

_____ 17. Apostrophes are used correctly with contractions and possessive nouns.

_____ 18. Commas or pairs of commas are used correctly.

_____ 19. Dialogue is punctuated and capitalized correctly.

_____ 20. Any correction that could not be rewritten/retyped is crossed out with a single line.

Record of Proofreading Corrections

Keeping a record of the kinds of mistakes you make can be helpful. For the next
few writing assignments, list the errors you, your teacher, or your peers find in
your work. If you faithfully use this kind of record, you'll find it easier to avoid
troublesome errors.

Writer's name _____ Title of paper _____

Write sentences that contain errors in grammar or usage here.   **Write corrections here.**

_____   _____

_____   _____

_____   _____

_____   _____

_____   _____

_____   _____

Write sentences that contain errors in mechanics here.   **Write corrections here.**

_____   _____

_____   _____

_____   _____

_____   _____

_____   _____

_____   _____

Write misspelled words and corrections here.

_____   _____   _____   _____

_____   _____   _____   _____

_____   _____   _____   _____

_____   _____   _____   _____

Multiple-Assignment Proofreading Record

When your teacher returns a corrected writing assignment, write the title or topic
on the appropriate vertical line in the right side of the chart. Under the title or
topic, record the number of errors you made in each area. Use this sheet when
you proofread your next assignment, taking care to check those areas in which
you make frequent mistakes.

Title or Topic of Assignment									
Type of Error									
Sentence Fragments									
Run-on Sentences									
Subject-Verb Agreement									
Pronoun Agreement									
Incorrect Pronoun Form									
Use of Double Negative									
Comparison of Adjectives and Adverbs									
Confusing Verbs									
Irregular Verbs									
Noun Plurals and Possessives									
Capitalization									
Spelling									
End Punctuation									
Apostrophes									
Confusing Words									
Quotation Marks and Italics									
Comma or Paired Commas									

My Writing and Speaking Records

Listening Self-Inventory

Questions and answers about my listening	More about my answers
What kinds of music do I like to listen to?	Why do I like them?
What TV shows and movies are my favorites?	What do I like about them?
How well do I listen in school?	How much do I learn by listening?
Do I listen carefully to what my friends say?	What do I learn from them?
When is it difficult for me to listen?	What makes it difficult?
How do I use the praise and suggestions of others to improve my skills?	How do I feel about getting praise or suggestions for improvement?

Speaking Self-Inventory

Questions and answers about my speaking	More about my answers
How do I feel about speaking to my friends?	What do I like to discuss with them?
How do I feel about talking to adults?	Why do I feel this way?
How do I feel about reciting or speaking to the class?	Why do I feel this way?
What is the most difficult thing about speaking?	Why is it difficult?
What techniques have I learned to improve my speaking?	How do I use these techniques with friends or in class?

My Writing Ideas

Clustering-Word Web

Fill in the center circle with a word related to your topic. Then fill in the other circles with related words or ideas. Add more circles, if necessary. Draw lines between the circles to show the connections.

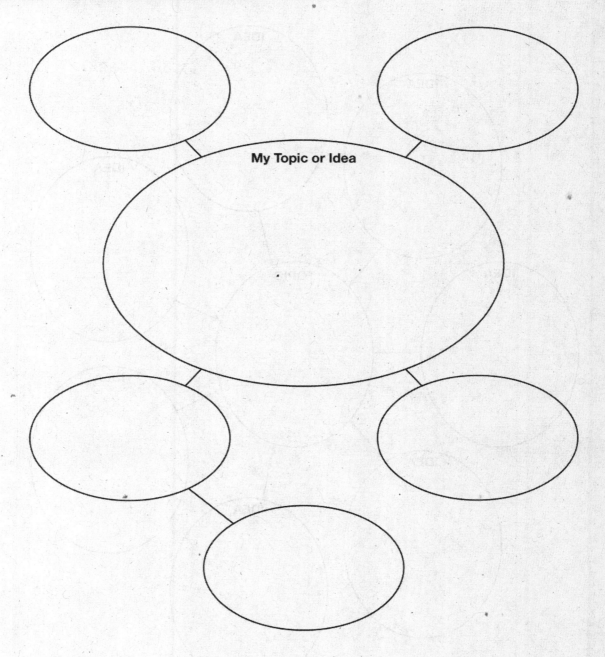

My Topic or Idea

Freeform Web

In the center circle, write a key word that identifies your topic. Then in the other circles, write ideas that relate to your topic. Don't take the time yet to consider how the ideas relate to each other.

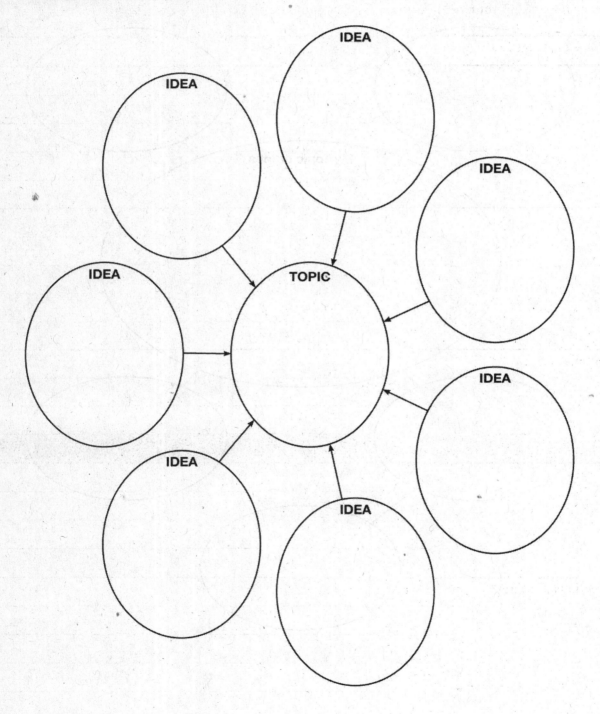

Sensory Details Chart

Think about the place or event you want to describe. On the lines below, write down all the sensory details you can recall. Use vivid language—colorful adjectives, precise nouns, expressive verbs. When you write your paper, include the details that will best help your readers "experience" that place or event with you.

Place or Event

Sights

_____
_____
_____
_____

Sounds

_____
_____
_____
_____

Smells

_____
_____
_____
_____

Tastes

_____
_____
_____

Feelings/Textures

_____
_____
_____
_____

Brainstorming-Freewriting

On the lines below, write about your topic for five minutes without stopping.
Write down every idea that comes into your head. After your time is up, reread
your ideas. Use a colored pencil or pen to circle or underline ideas that you want
to develop in your paper.

_____

_____

_____

_____

_____

_____

_____

_____

_____

_____

_____

_____

_____

_____

_____

_____

_____

_____

_____

_____

Using an Outline

In the outline below, first write your main idea or opinion statement. Next, write three major reasons on which you base your main idea or opinion. Below each reason, write your supporting details or information. Try to elaborate on each item of support. For example, how does the supporting information prove your point? Finally, write your summary statement.

Main Idea or Opinion Statement:

_____

_____

Reason #1:_____

    Supporting Detail #1 _____

    Elaboration: _____

    Supporting Detail #2 _____

    Elaboration: _____

Reason #2:_____

    Supporting Detail #1 _____

    Elaboration: _____

    Supporting Detail #2 _____

    Elaboration: _____

Reason #3:_____

    Supporting Detail #1 _____

    Elaboration: _____

    Supporting Detail #2 _____

    Elaboration: _____

Summing It Up:

_____

_____

_____

My Listening Notes
and Speaking Ideas

My Listening Notes

Speaker's name: _____

Topic: _____

Purpose: _____

Main Ideas	Notes

Speaker's name: _____

Topic: _____

Purpose: _____

Main Ideas	Notes

My Listening Notes

Speaker's name: _____

Topic: _____

Purpose: _____

Main Ideas	Notes

Speaker's name: _____

Topic: _____

Purpose: _____

Main Ideas	Notes

Speaker's name: _____

Topic: _____

Purpose: _____

Main Ideas	Notes

My Speaking Ideas

Assignment	
Topic	
Audience	
Purpose	

Ideas

My Speaking Ideas

Assignment	
Topic	
Audience	
Purpose	

Ideas

Assignment	
Topic	
Audience	
Purpose	

Ideas

Assignment	
Topic	
Audience	
Purpose	

Ideas

Assignment	
Topic	
Audience	
Purpose	

Ideas

My Writing Workshops

Prewriting: Editorial Writing Prompts

Choose your own issue for your editorial, or use one of the following prompts.

WORKPLACE

Federal legislation states that teenagers may be paid a reduced minimum wage during their first ninety days of employment. Write an editorial outlining your argument for or against this legislation. Be sure to support your opinion statement with logical appeals as well as appeals to emotions and ethics. Submit your editorial to a local newspaper.

SCHOOL

Your school has decided to adopt a closed-campus policy, requiring that students remain on campus during lunch. The administration believes that this policy will cut down on tardiness, reduce traffic problems, and give students more time to eat. Write an editorial for your school newspaper arguing for or against the school's decision to close campus.

ATHLETICS

A sports team at your high school recently lost some key players because of poor grades. The players have been removed from the team until their grades improve. The team may lose some upcoming games without these players. However, many in the community feel that academics should be put before athletics. Write an editorial to your school board arguing for or against the decision to remove the players from the team.

JOURNALISM

Many staff members of the school newspaper feel that they should be allowed more independence in choosing and editing the stories that appear in the paper. Draft an editorial for your school newspaper arguing for or against greater student control of the paper's content.

WORLD LANGUAGES

Your school requires at least two years of study of a second language in order to graduate. However, some people feel that only college-bound students should have to meet this requirement. Write an editorial for your local newspaper arguing for or against this policy.

Prewriting: Issue, Thesis, and Support

Use the chart below to help you plan your editorial. Use additional paper if necessary.

- List three issues in the chart. Rate them based on the questions and select the issue with the highest total points.

- What is your position? Jot down a thesis statement and one or two sentences that identify the issue and state your perspective.

- List at least three reasons for your opinion. Then, provide precise and relevant supporting evidence—facts, examples, anecdotes, expert opinions, or cause-effect reasoning—and any elaboration if needed. Keep in mind the types of appeals you will use to make your argument.

ISSUE RATINGS CHART
(Rate each issue from 1 to 5 on the considerations—5 being the highest)

Considerations	Issue 1:	Issue 2:	Issue 3:
Is the issue narrow enough to be argued in a short editorial?			
Can each side make a good case for its position?			
Do people have strong feelings about the issue?			
	Total:	Total:	Total:

THESIS:

SUPPORT

Reason 1:	Reason 2:	Reason 3:
Evidence:	Evidence:	Evidence:
Elaboration:	Elaboration:	Elaboration:

Writing Workshop

Drafting: Organizing and Writing Your Editorial

Complete the graphic organizer below, and use it to help you write your first draft. Use additional paper if necessary.

INTRODUCTION

Attention-grabbing statement:
Background information on the issue:
Thesis statement:

BODY

Second-strongest reason:	Third-strongest reason:	Strongest reason:
Evidence:	Evidence:	Evidence:

CONCLUSION

Restatement of opinion and reasons:
Call to action:

Writing Workshop

Evaluating: Student Model Think Sheet

Answer the questions below to get a better understanding of the structure of an editorial. Use additional paper if necessary.

- Re-read "Safe Teen Driving." The notes in the margin will help you identify important elements of an editorial.

- As you respond to the questions, think about the use of language, the organization of information, and the strategies used for developing ideas and elaborating on them.

QUESTIONS AND RESPONSES

1. What issue is discussed in the editorial?

_____

_____

_____

2. What opinion is expressed about the issue?

_____

_____

_____

3. What reason best supports the thesis statement? Why?

_____

_____

_____

4. What types of evidence does the editorial use to support its reasons?

_____

_____

_____

5. What action does the editorial encourage readers to take?

_____

_____

_____

Writing Workshop

Evaluating: Editorials

Use the following questions to evaluate your editorial or that of one of your classmates.

- Make brief notes to answer the questions.
- Rate the parts of the editorial. The lowest score is **1,** and the highest is **4.**
- Make at least three suggestions for improving the editorial.

1. Does the introduction grab the reader's attention?

   Rating: 1 2 3 4

   Suggestion: _____

2. Does the thesis statement clearly state the position?

   Rating: 1 2 3 4

   Suggestion: _____

3. Are there at least three convincing reasons? Are they supported by evidence?

   Rating: 1 2 3 4

   Suggestion: _____

4. Are the reasons organized in a manner that aids the editorial's persuasiveness?

   Rating: 1 2 3 4

   Suggestion: _____

5. Are rhetorical devices used? Are they effective?

   Rating: 1 2 3 4

   Suggestion: _____

6. Does the conclusion restate the opinion, summarize the reasons, and include a call to action?

   Rating: 1 2 3 4

   Suggestion: _____

Writing Workshop

Revising: Improve Your Editorial

Use the rubric in this chart to help you improve your editorial.

Questions	Do This	Changes You Made
1. Does the introduction grab the reader's attention and include background information?	_____**Circle** the question, detail, or anecdote that would grab the reader's interest. _____**Put a star** by any background information.	
2. Does the introduction contain a clear opinion statement?	_____**Underline** the opinion statement.	
3. Are at least three reasons provided? What types of appeals are used?	_____**Highlight** each reason. _____**Write** the types of appeals in the margin.	
4. Is each reason supported by relevant evidence?	_____**Box** each piece of evidence. _____**Draw an arrow** from each item to the reason it supports.	
5. Are the reasons organized effectively?	_____**Number** the reasons from strongest to weakest. If the order seems illogical or ineffective, revise.	
6. Are rhetorical devices used effectively?	_____**Underline** any uses of repetition, rhetorical questions, or parallelism that enhance the argument.	
7. Is the opinion restated in the conclusion? Is there a call to action?	_____**Underline** the sentence that restates the opinion. _____**Put a check mark** next to sentences that make a call to action.	

Proofreading Checklist

GUIDELINES FOR PROOFREADING	Yes	No	Needs Work
Is every sentence complete, not a fragment or a run-on?			
Are punctuation marks—such as end marks, commas, semicolons, colons, dashes, and quotation marks—used correctly?			
Are proper nouns, proper adjectives, and the first words of sentences capitalized?			
Does every verb agree in number with its subject?			
Are verbs and tenses used correctly?			
Are subject and object forms of personal pronouns used correctly?			
Does every pronoun agree with its antecedent in number and in gender? Are pronoun references clear?			
Are frequently confused words (such as *fewer* and *less, affect* and *effect*) used correctly?			
Are all words spelled correctly? Are the plural forms of words correct?			
Is the paper neat and correct in form?			

Writing Workshop

Framework for Editorials

Use the following framework to help you evaluate your own writing and the models on the following pages.

- Focuses on an **issue of personal importance**
- Shows **why the issue is important**
- Presents arguments and ideas in a **logical, organized** way
- Uses **reasoning and evidence** that readers will respond to
- **Addresses potential concerns, biases**, and **counterclaims** readers may have
- Uses **rhetorical devices**
- **Motivates readers** to consider their own point of view on the issue and perhaps take action

Writing Workshop

Editorial: Score Point 4

Read the student model below. With the Framework as a guide, write an evaluation of the model in the commentary box, explaining why the model received the score shown above.

Model	Commentary
As I near the school cafeteria I'm bombarded by the fragrant aromas of today's lunch. Top on the menu are tougher-than-leather hamburger patties and greasy French fries. Of course, instead of the fries, I can opt for lumpy mashed potatoes made from dried flakes or choose soggy, overcooked canned vegetables. And for dessert I'll have my pick of an assortment of baked goods loaded with white flour and sugar—or some kind of scary-looking Jell-o mold. This is nutritious? I've had it! What this school needs more than anything else is a salad bar.	
Today in the 21st century salad bars are springing up in school lunchrooms from Lodi, California, to Chicago, Illinois, to Syracuse, New York. So why not here? Imagine being able to put together a fresh salad of leafy green lettuce, juicy tomatoes, and cucumbers. Or a fruit salad with raspberry yogurt and trail mix? If you're a minimalist, you might enjoy cheese and grapes with a granola bar. For dessert, why not a juicy apple instead of calorie-rich apple pie? Wouldn't it be great to come away from lunch feeling energetic and aware instead of dull and stuffed to the gills?	
It's too expensive to install a salad bar, some will no doubt argue. But guess what? According to statistics from the Centers for Disease Control, about 18 percent of kids from 12 to 19 are overweight. And across the country, a total of 58 million people have more poundage than is healthy. Another 40 million have gone beyond being merely overweight to joining the ranks of the obese. Overweight can lead to serious health problems up the road, so if you think about it, it costs more in human health to not have a salad bar. If we want to reduce costs, why not add an extra dollar to everyone's annual school fees. Even better, we could create our own garden on school grounds. Then we'd get the pleasure that comes from eating ultra-local produce we've grown ourselves.	
Anyone who wants to should of course feel free to slurp up the spaghetti and meatballs or this week's variety of mystery meats. But the administrators should give serious consideration to this idea for us who want salad. I say, let's get this school on the "crunch lunch" bandwagon—now!	

Editorial: Score Point 3

Read the student model below. With the Framework as a guide,
write an evaluation of the model in the commentary box,
explaining why the model received the score shown above.

Model	Commentary
As I near the school cafeteria I can smell today's lunch and I already know it's not that good. We're having hamburgers and greasy French fries. Then there'll be the usual soggy vegetables and other unapetizing things. No matter what you get in the hot food line on any day, it doesn't quite live up to the title of fresh. I say we need to put a salad bar in this school cafeteria, like yesterday.	
Here's my reasons. First of all, it's a known fact that a lot of schools already have salad bars. They have all the usual ingredients you'd get if you went to a restaurant and had salad bar there—fresh fruits and vegetables in other words. When was the last time we had a salad in this place that wasn't made from wilting iceburg lettuce? We both know, teachers and students, that this isn't what we want to eat for lunch ever day. Imagine fresh greens and other good things. I think a lot of kids would rather eat these things than mystery meat.	
I can already hear some people complaining it'll cost too much to have a salad bar. Nuts! Or that it's unsannitary. For one thing, the salad bar has that thick plexiglass covering for a reason—to keep out germs from sneezing and coughing kids. Also, not having a salad bar is a risk that kids will gain a lot of weight eating junk food at school. Did you know that about 18 percent of teens in this country are overweight? And being overweight can lead to serious health problems later on. By having a salad bar we are lessning the risk that we get fat to.	
To pay for it we could add a dollar onto the annual school fees just for the salad bar. We could also grow our own garden right on these school grounds. I think people who grow their own food care more about eating it. I know I would, if I grew my own food.	
So the bottom line is, if you like eating mystery meat every day, that's fine. But what about us kids who'd like a break? I say please give it a shot. You'll make a lot of kids happy by giving us a little fresh lettuce and tomatoes.	

Writing Workshop

Editorial: Score Point 2

Read the student model below. With the Framework as a guide, write an evaluation of the model in the commentary box, explaining why the model received the score shown above.

Model	Commentary
The other day I had a thought about something that was missing at my school. It's a salad bar. Other schools have them so why not here? My dads a doctor and he recently told me that thear are alot of overweight teens in this country. I know this is true because I've seen it with my own eyes. So why don't we just get a salad bar. It would give me and some others some other good things to eat besides helping wieght problems. It's boring to eat the same old hamburgers and greazy french fries most of the time. I think other kids think this too. Actualy I can formally state the reason it is important to have a salad bar. A salad bar gives people alot of good fresh foods to eat. I know people young and old eat from salad bars. I went to a restaurant last night that had them. People were lined up to get at that thing. Too many people make a fuss over the food in this cafeteria. But they have a problem with getting a salad bar in there. Officially speaking, it's what teachers and adults want kids to eat. They want a healthy diet. This would help me and other people have that. Okay so some people think public salad bar is full of germs. This isn't true at all. My dad showed me that the reason for those plastic things above the salad are to keep out germs. So I'm not afraid to eat at a salad bar at all. Niether should anyone else be. And how much extra money could it cost to have some lettuce? Is that a crazy thought or what. Having a salad probly costs less than the hamburger lunch. Bring in the salad bar. Make people happy. Make people healthy. Doctors would thank you. And if your reading this then you might want to think about having a salad bar at school too.	

Writing Workshop

Practice with Conventions

Circle the letter of the best answer to each of the following items.
(40 points; 4 points each)

1. **Which sentence shows correct punctuation?**

   A) It was, he said "as beautiful a moment as one can imagine."

   B) "Barry," she asked, "Have you called your mother today?"

   C) "That child," he whispered, "is simply amazing to watch."

   D) Then they all walked away and yelled "We will!"

2. **Which version of the sentence is grammatically correct?**

   A) Every one of the pets have been properly trained.

   B) Every one of the pets has been properly trained.

   C) Everyone of the pets has been properly trained.

   D) Everyone of the pets have been properly trained.

3. **Which word is spelled correctly?**

   A) collossal

   B) etiquete

   C) minimum

   D tarriff

4. **Which version of the sentence shows correct punctuation?**

   A) Peter's favorite novel is Ernest Hemingway's Farewell to Arms.

   B) Peter's favorite novel is Ernest Hemingway's *Farewell to Arms*.

   C) Peter's favorite novel is Ernest Hemingway's "Farewell to Arms."

   D) Peter's favorite novel is Ernest Hemingway's *"Farewell to Arms."*

5. **Which word is spelled incorrectly?**

   A) cordially

   B) mentioned

   C) sieze

   D) valuable

6. **Which version of the sentence shows correct capitalization?**

   A) The Lincoln memorial in Washington, D.C., is open on Holidays.

   B) The Lincoln Memorial in Washington, D.C., is open on holidays.

   C) The Lincoln Memorial in Washington, D.C., is open on Holidays.

   D) The Lincoln memorial in washington, D.C., is open on holidays.

7. Which word is spelled incorrectly?

A) environment

B) genius

C) inevitable

D) permanent

8. Which version of the sentence shows correct capitalization?

A) Donna bought two Cans of Perfect Paint at Drake hardware in Bloomington.

B) Donna bought two cans of Perfect Paint at drake hardware in bloomington.

C) Donna bought two cans of Perfect Paint at Drake Hardware in Bloomington.

D) Donna bought two Cans of Perfect paint at drake Hardware in Bloomington.

9. Imelda is adding a <u>line graph</u> to her editorial. What should the line graph include?

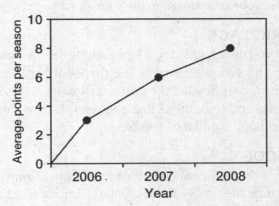

A) a title

B) a colored line

C) graphics

D) percentages

10. Which version of the sentence is grammatically correct?

A) Dan, the youngest in the family, is clearly the most imaginative.

B) Dan the youngest in the family, is clearly the most imaginative.

C) Dan, the youngest in the family is clearly the most imaginative.

D) Dan, the youngest, in the family, is clearly the most imaginative.

Prewriting: Short Story Writing Prompts

Choose your own situation for your short story, or use one of the following prompts.

WORKPLACE

Have you ever had a day when nothing seemed to go right? Write a short story in which a character arrives late for his or her first day at a new job due to circumstances beyond the character's control. Be sure to consider the potential conflicts and resolutions that could result from this situation. Share your story with your school's guidance counselor.

SCHOOL

Write a short story about a character whose family must move on a regular basis. Each time the family moves, your character must leave his or her friends behind. In your story, explore the experience of attending school under such circumstances. Share your story with a friend who has had to change schools.

PHYSICAL EDUCATION

Write a short story about a character's experiences while climbing a mountain, running a marathon, playing in a championship football game, or any other sports activity. Use flashbacks to show the important experiences that have shaped the character up to this point. Keep your readers' interest by including problems and conflicts that the character has to overcome. Share your story with a classmate who is interested in the challenges.

HISTORY

Write a story in which a character meets a famous person in history, such as a world leader, an influential author, or an important scientist. Create the circumstances under which they meet, and describe what happens during and after the meeting. Be sure to consider the central conflict that will drive the events of your story. Let your history teacher read the story.

LANGUAGE ARTS

Write a modern version of a classic story you have read. For example, you might write an updated version of the Cinderella fairy tale. Be sure to make your characters realistic, and consider how modern circumstances would affect their personalities. In addition, decide whether the plot would remain the same or if it would change due to the present-day setting. Share your story with your school's librarian.

Writing Workshop

Prewriting: Situation, Characters, and Plot

Use the graphic organizers on these two pages to plan your short story. Use additional paper if necessary.

- List a few observations and a "What if . . . ?" question about each observation.
- Then, choose the story idea that you think will make the most interesting short story.
- Use concrete sensory details to answer the questions about characters and to describe the sights, sounds, and smells of your story's setting.
- Answer the questions in the flowchart to develop your plot. Then, choose the point of view from which you will write your short story, and list examples of stylistic devices you will use.

SITUATION

Observations	What if . . . ? (story ideas)
News stories:	
Interesting-looking people:	
Everyday situations:	
Story idea I will use:	

CHARACTERS

	What is the character's appearance?	How does the character behave?	What motivates the character?
Main character(s):			
Secondary character(s):			

SETTING

	Sights	Sounds	Smells
Where:			
When:			

PLOT

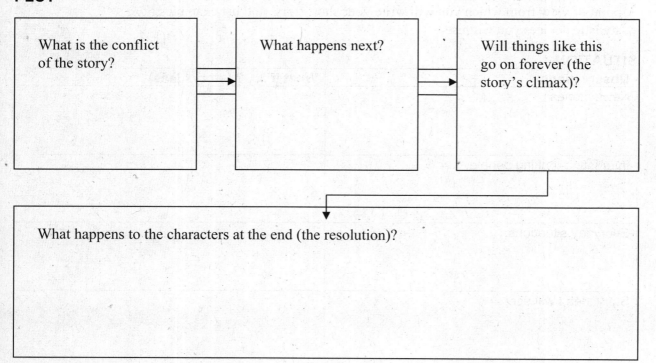

What is the conflict of the story?

What happens next?

Will things like this go on forever (the story's climax)?

What happens to the characters at the end (the resolution)?

POINT OF VIEW (Circle one)

First person   Third-person limited   Third-person omniscient

STYLISTIC DEVICES

Figures of speech (similes, metaphors, personification):	Imagery:	Irony:

Drafting: Organizing and Writing Your Short Story

**Complete the graphic organizer below, and use it to help plan your first draft.
Use additional paper if necessary.**

BEGINNING

Attention getter:	
Setting:	
Main character(s):	
Point of view:	
Conflict:	

MIDDLE

Events leading to climax (plot complications):	Dialogue and other important details:

END

Climax:
Resolution of conflict:
Final outcome:
Significance of events:

Writing Workshop

Evaluating: Student Model Think Sheet

Answer the questions below to get a better understanding of the structure of a short story. Use additional paper if necessary.

- Re-read "The Discovery." The notes in the margin will help you identify important elements of a short story.

- As you respond to the questions, think about the use of language, the story's organization, and the strategies used for developing the characters, setting, and plot.

QUESTIONS AND RESPONSES

1. Where does the story take place?

   _____

   _____

2. Who is the main character?

   _____

   _____

3. What conflict does the main character face?

   _____

   _____

4. What is the final outcome?

   _____

   _____

   _____

5. What stylistic devices are used?

   _____

   _____

   _____

6. Does anything else catch your interest or seem important? In what way?

   _____

   _____

   _____

Evaluating: Short Stories

Use the following questions to evaluate your short story or that of one of your classmates.

- Make brief notes to answer the questions.
- Rate the parts of the short story. The lowest score is **1,** and the highest is **4.**
- Make at least three suggestions for improving the short story.

1. Choose one element (character, conflict, setting) and tell whether this information has been provided.

   Rating: 1 2 3 4

   Suggestion: _____

2. What is the point of view? Is it developed consistently?

   Rating: 1 2 3 4

   Suggestion: _____

3. How well do complications help develop the plot?

   Rating: 1 2 3 4

   Suggestion: _____

4. Choose one detail (transitional words or phrases, dialogue, interior monologue, concrete sensory details) and explain how it helps create a character or advance the plot.

   Rating: 1 2 3 4

   Suggestion: _____

5. Are stylistic devices used in the short story? Give an example of either a figure of speech, imagery, or irony.

   Rating: 1 2 3 4

   Suggestion: _____

6. What is the story's climax? How is the conflict resolved?

   Rating: 1 2 3 4

   Suggestion: _____

Revising: Improve Your Short Story

Use the rubric in this chart to help you improve your short story.

QUESTIONS	DO THIS	CHANGES YOU MADE
1. Does the beginning name the main character(s) and start the conflict? Does it give vivid details about the setting?	_____**Draw** a box around the name(s) of the main character(s). _____**Highlight** the event or situation that starts the conflict. _____**Bracket** details of the setting.	
2. Does the story have a clear point of view? Is the point of view developed consistently?	_____**Label** the point of view in the margin with **1** for first person, **3L** for third-person limited, or **3O** for third-person omniscient. _____**Underline** the point of view.	
3. Is the plot developed with complications shown by specific actions and events?	_____**Number** each plot complication and, in the margin, label the complication as a specific action or an event.	
4. Does the story use dialogue, interior monologue, and concrete sensory details to create complex characters?	_____**Draw a dotted line** under characters' words or thoughts. _____**Put parentheses** around concrete sensory details.	
5. Does the story use stylistic devices?	_____**Circle** each figure of speech, use of imagery, or use of irony.	
6. Does the end include a climax? Does it resolve the story's conflict and show the significance of the events?	_____**Put a star** by the climax. _____**Bracket** the resolution. _____**Highlight** the significance of the events.	
7. Do transitions advance the plot? Are quotes punctuated correctly?	_____**Bracket** all transitions that advance the plot. _____**Put a check** by incorrectly punctuated quotes.	

Writing Workshop

Proofreading Checklist

GUIDELINES FOR PROOFREADING	Yes	No	Needs Work
Is every sentence complete, not a fragment or a run-on?			
Are punctuation marks—such as end marks, commas, semicolons, colons, dashes, and quotation marks—used correctly?			
Are proper nouns, proper adjectives, and the first words of sentences capitalized?			
Does every verb agree in number with its subject?			
Are verbs and tenses used correctly?			
Are subject and object forms of personal pronouns used correctly?			
Does every pronoun agree with its antecedent in number and in gender? Are pronoun references clear?			
Are frequently confused words (such as *fewer* and *less, affect* and *effect*) used correctly?			
Are all words spelled correctly? Are the plural forms of words correct?			
Is the paper neat and correct in form?			

Framework for Short Stories

**Use the following framework to help you evaluate your own writing
and the models on the following pages.**

- Introduces complex, interesting **characters**
- Begins with a **conflict** that builds to a **climax** and ends in **resolution**
- Locates **scenes and actions** in specific, vivid settings
- Presents a clear and consistent **point of view**
- **Dialogue** enhances **plot** and adds to **character development**
- Uses **concrete narrative details** and **sensory** (sight, sound, touch, smell, taste) **details**
- Uses **interior monologue** to convey character's thoughts and feelings
- Uses **figurative language** and other devices to enhance style

Short Story: Score Point 4

Read the student model below. With the Framework as a guide, write an evaluation of the model in the commentary box, explaining why the model received the score shown above.

Model	Commentary
Dawg was done. Just thinking about it choked me up a bit. It was our last few moments together, parked there in my car. Then I'd let him go. For good. I looked at Dawg settled easily beside me in the passenger seat. His brown eyes seemed to stare me down with trust and love, like he had no idea this was the end for us. I looked away, out the window, feeling a complicated mix of melancholy, regret, and excitement.	
Rain was pelting the roof now. Distant thunderclouds rose into the sky like huge, purple pillows. The storm was building, just like the one inside me.	
"This is it, Lucky Dawg," I said, laying my hand oh his hard, warm skull. "Can't help it."	
Dawg's mouth opened, like he was smiling at me. I felt that old familiar appreciation. Lucky Dawg was no pure breed. He was a German shepherd-Lab mix as far as I could tell. But he was one smart dog. He could learn in hours what I imagined other dogs took days to understand. But there'd be others for me, I knew, and I'd eventually have to let them go, too.	
As the rain came harder, I suddenly imagined myself pulling away from the curb, flipping a hard U-turn, and racing back home, Dawg and me. I could pretend this didn't have to happen. I would! What difference would one more day make?	
Quickly I started the car again. The engine hummed and I pulled out into the empty, rain-sloshed street. Then a giant clap of thunder cracked the sky. Dawg sat up. His tail thumped the seat eagerly. I sighed and shook my head. Who was I kidding? Dawg had to go.	
In only a few minutes we were there. I opened the car door and Dawg bounded out and up the steps to the tall, thin man standing on his front porch.	
"Lucky Dawg!" Sam said. His hand reached out and fumbled for Dawg's head. "I heard you coming!"	
"He's all yours now, Sam," I said, guiding his hand to Dawg's harness. "You two stay out of mischief, huh?"	
Sam chuckled. "Don't count on it," he replied. "This may be the first seeing-eye dog you've ever trained, Matt, but I think Dawg here has learned how to have plenty of fun."	

Writing Workshop EXTENSION

Short Story: Score Point 3

Read the student model below. With the Framework as a guide, write an evaluation of the model in the commentary box, explaining why the model received the score shown above.

Model	Commentary
I was feeling bad about my dog. Well he wasnt totally my dog. But then again he was. But after all this time with old Lucky Dawg, I wasn't feeling to lucky. He had to go. Today was the day. But at the same time, as I drove along with him beside me, I couldn't help wanting to turn back.	
Outside the car, dark thunderclouds were building. They didn't bother Dawg. He was more interested in barking at things. But those clouds meant a storm was coming, just like the one building in me.	
"This is it, Dawg," I said to him as we neared our destenation. "Can't help it. This is just the way it has to be." He looked over at me with his brown eyes full of trust and love, like he didn't know this was the end for us. But of course, how would he?	
The rain was starting to really pelt down now. I put my hand on Dawg's smooth, hard head, appreciating him. He was no purebred dog, just a mix of German Sheperd and Lab. But he was smart! He learned really fast all the things I imagined other dogs would take weeks to learn. But now it was all over.	
As we drove up the lane, Dawg's tail began to beat excitedly on the seat. But the rain wasn't helping my mood. Suddenly I imagined turning the car around and roaring off, Dawg beside me, our mission forgotten. I slowed the car, looking for a place to make a U-turn. But then a giant clap of thunder rocked me back to my senses. I drove on, straight ahead.	
When we got there, Sam was waiting for us on his inclosed porch. Dawg bounded out of the car and up the steps. Sam fumbled to find Dawg's head and petted him. Sam had been blind for five years, but this was his first seeing-eye dog. My first as a trainer, too.	
"I heard you coming, Matt," Sam said.	
"Lucky Dawg's all yours now, Sam!" I replied. We both smiled, even though I felt a little sad. But Sam had Lucky Dawg to keep him company now. And the next day I'd begin training a new dog. So things were really pretty good.	

Writing Workshop

Short Story: Score Point 2

Read the student model below. With the Framework as a guide, write an evaluation of the model in the commentary box, explaining why the model received the score shown above.

Model	Commentary
One day I was really upset. I had to take the dog I'd been training and give him to his new owner. I'd been around him, named Lucky Dawg, since he was a puppy. I thought he was a mix of a German shepherd and a Lab. He was just the kind of dog I'd like to have for my own. But that wasn't my job. I had to give him away that day.	
Of course I was happy for Sam, the guy who was getting Dawg. Sam needed Dawg to help him get places because his eyes had been seriously injured in a fire a few years ago, and now he couldnt see. One thing I knew was, Sam was getting the best dog ever.	
That made my mood complicated. I both was happy for Sam and not so happy for me. Also, it was rainig. Rain can get to you, especially when its hard rain and thundering like it was that day. It made me just want to stay inside instead of having to drive all the way to Sam's place.	
But we got in the car and headed of. "Don't worry, Dawg," I maneged to say, "you're going to have a great new home."	
Dawg barked like he totally understood me. That's how smart this dog is. But the closer we got to Sam's, the slower I started driving. For a while there I imagined just not going at all. In fact, I put on my blinker at one point and started looking for a place to do a U-turn. But the rain was so hard that it was hard to even see out the windsheild. Just when I was about to make the turn around, a huge clap of thunder slamed the sky. Whoa! I thought maybe it was a sign. I wised up and just kept driving forward.	
"Glad you finally made it," Sam said when we pulled up in front of his house and Dawg and I got out of the car. "I heard you coming."	
He reached out and petted Dawg. Then he grabbed his harness. Lucky Dawg was all Sams now.	
"Good luck," I said. I thought I'd come visit them again some day, so I ended up feeling alright in the end.	

Practice with Conventions

Circle the letter of the best answer to each of the following items.
(40 points; 4 points each)

1. Which word is spelled incorrectly?

   A) heroes

   B) labratory

   C) maneuver

   D) recognize

2. Which version of the sentence shows correct capitalization?

   A) Mandy's Favorite Writer, James Michener, wrote a novel set in Hawaii.

   B) Mandy's favorite writer, James michener, wrote a novel set in Hawaii.

   C) Mandy's favorite writer, James Michener, wrote a novel set in Hawaii.

   D) mandy's favorite Writer, James Michener, wrote a novel set in Hawaii.

3. Read this sentence.

   > Her goals were to clearly speak;
   > overwhelmingly convince the
   > judges.

   How should the underlined portion be written?

   A) speak clearly and to convince the judges overwhelmingly

   B) clearly speak and to convince the judges overwhelmingly

   C) clearly speak and to overwhelmingly convince the judges

   D) speak clearly and to overwhelmingly convince the judges

4. Which version of the sentence shows correct punctuation?

   A) I was told to buy three of each of the following; pens, pencils, erasers.

   B) I was told to buy three of each of the following: pens, pencils, erasers.

   C) I was told to buy three of each of the following: pens, pencils, and erasers.

   D) I was told to buy three of each of the following, pens, pencils, and erasers.

5. Which word is spelled correctly?

   A) suppres

   B) suppress

   C) supres

   D supress

6. Which version of the sentence is grammatically correct?

   A) Dawn and I visited the orphanage.

   B) Dawn and myself visited the orphanage.

   C) Dawn and I myself visited the orphanage.

   D) Dawn and we ourselves visited the orphanage.

7. Which word is spelled correctly?

A) persue

B) shiney

C) thoroughly

D) twelth

8. Which version of the sentence shows correct punctuation?

A) The game was long and boring, nevertheless, Mario kept watching.

B) The game was long and boring: nevertheless, Mario kept watching.

C) The game was long and boring— nevertheless—Mario kept watching.

D) The game was long and boring; nevertheless, Mario kept watching.

9. Read this sentence.

> Do you recall who wrote the short story <u>The Celebrated Jumping Frog of Calaveras County</u>?

How should the underlined portion be written?

A) *The Celebrated Jumping Frog of Calaveras County*

B) "The Celebrated Jumping Frog of Calaveras County"

C) The Celebrated Jumping Frog Of Calaveras County

D) the *Celebrated Jumping Frog of Calaveras County*

10. Which version of the sentence shows correct capitalization?

A) The Illinois state fair takes place in Springfield, the state's capital.

B) The Illinois State Fair takes place in Springfield, the state's capital.

C) The Illinois State Fair takes place in Springfield, the state's Capital.

D) The Illinois state fair takes place in Springfield, the state's Capital.

My Writing Workshops

Prewriting: Historical Investigation Report Writing Prompts

Choose your own issue for your historical investigation report, or use one of the following prompts.

WORKPLACE

When choosing a career, people are frequently influenced by those whose work they admire. They may turn to scientists such as Albert Einstein or Marie Curie as role models. They may seek inspiration from leaders like Thomas Jefferson or Dr. Martin Luther King, Jr. In a historical investigation report, synthesize various points of view about a person in history who became famous for work in a career that interests you. Address your report to people who are also interested in this type of career.

SCHOOL

From Greek philosopher and teacher Socrates to American math teacher Jaime Escalante, teachers have influenced and inspired the people of their day and left their mark on history itself. Using a variety of points of view, write a historical investigation report on the educational approach of a famous teacher. Address your paper to an audience of your peers.

WORLD LANGUAGE

Many languages have "family trees" that can be traced into the past. English, for example, has Latin roots and Germanic and French influences as a result of the intermingling of cultures through migration and invasion. Research a language you are studying or one that interests you. Consult a number of sources that represent different points of view, and write a historical investigation report on the historical events and peoples that have shaped the way the language is spoken today. Address your report to a world language class.

SCIENCE

Isaac Newton and his apple, Ben Franklin and his kite—many people are familiar with the stories of how these two scientists made their respective discoveries about gravity and electricity. Synthesizing a variety of points of view, write a historical investigation report about the story of a famous scientist's most important discovery. Address the report to members of your science class.

HISTORY

Did George Washington really chop down a cherry tree? Did Betsy Ross really sew the first American flag? Some stories are actually historical myths that may have a grain of truth in them but have been exaggerated or embellished over time. Choose a historical event to investigate, and write a historical investigation report substantiating or refuting the facts of the event by consulting sources that represent different points of view. Share your report with family or friends.

Writing Workshop

Prewriting: Choose and Research a Topic

Use the graphic organizer below to help you choose a topic and begin preliminary research of a historical event. Use additional paper if necessary.

- Answer the questions below to help you find and narrow a topic for your research.
- Then, write a list of questions to help focus your research. As you gather sources, keep a balance between primary and secondary sources as well as varying perspectives.

CHOOSE A TOPIC

What historical event interests me?
How can I narrow this topic, if necessary?
Can I find a variety of sources on this topic? List some possible sources.
Can I find sources representing all relevant perspectives on this topic? What are the relevant perspectives?
My topic:

RESEARCH QUESTIONS

Questions:	Specific Sources:
1.	 Relevant Perspective: (Circle one) Primary Secondary
2.	 Relevant Perspective: (Circle one) Primary Secondary
3.	 Relevant Perspective: (Circle one) Primary Secondary
4.	 Relevant Perspective: (Circle one) Primary Secondary

My Writing Workshops

Prewriting: Write a Thesis/Make an Outline

Use the graphic organizers below to write a thesis statement and start developing a formal outline. Use additional paper if necessary.

- Document your sources according to the appropriate style guide (MLA or APA) and compile a *Works Cited* page.

WRITE A THESIS STATEMENT:

My topic or how all my information fits together:		My conclusion about my research:		Thesis statement:
	+		**=**	

DEVELOP AN OUTLINE:

(Circle the best way to order your information)

Chronological order	Logical order	Order of importance

I. Introduction

   A. Overview of research:

   B. Thesis statement:

II.

   A.

     1.

     2

     3.

   B.

     1.

     2.

     3.

Writing Workshop

Drafting: Organizing and Writing Your Report

Complete the graphic organizer below, and use it to help you write your first draft. Use additional paper if necessary.

INTRODUCTION

Interesting opener:
Background information/overview of research:
Thesis statement:

BODY

First main idea:	Second main idea:	Third main idea:
Support:	Support:	Support:

CONCLUSION

Restatement of thesis and summary of main points:
Concluding thought or thought-provoking idea:

WORKS CITED

Source 1:
Source 2:
Source 3:

Evaluating: Student Model Think Sheet

Answer the questions below to get a better understanding of the structure of a historical investigation report. Use additional paper if necessary.

- Re-read "Sherman's March: A Civil War Controversy." The notes in the margin will help you identify important elements of a historical investigation report.

- As you respond to the questions, think about the use of language, the organization of information, and the strategies used for developing ideas and elaborating on them.

QUESTIONS AND RESPONSES

1. Does the overview of the research seem complete in the introduction?

_____

_____

2. Which main idea best supports the thesis?

_____

_____

3. Which citation (a direct quotation, a summary, or a paraphrase) is the most convincing?

_____

_____

4. Does the conclusion accurately restate the thesis?

_____

_____

5. Does anything else catch your interest or seem important? In what way?

_____

_____

_____

Evaluating: Historical Investigation Reports

Use the following questions to evaluate your historical investigation report or that of one of your classmates.

- Make brief notes to answer the questions.
- Rate the parts of the historical investigation. The lowest score is **1,** and the highest is **4.**
- Make at least three suggestions for improving the historical investigation.

1. Does the introduction grab the reader's attention, give an overview of the research, and include a thesis statement?

   Rating: 1 2 3 4

   Suggestion: _____

2. Do several main ideas develop the thesis statement?

   Rating: 1 2 3 4

   Suggestion: _____

3. Are the main ideas supported by facts and details?

   Rating: 1 2 3 4

   Suggestion: _____

4. Does the report include summaries and paraphrases as well as direct quotations?

   Rating: 1 2 3 4

   Suggestion: _____

5. Are all sources cited when necessary? Are they formatted correctly?

   Rating: 1 2 3 4

   Suggestion: _____

6. Does the conclusion restate the thesis, summarize the main ideas, and include a final thought?

   Rating: 1 2 3 4

   Suggestion: _____

Revising: Improve Your Historical Investigation Report

Use the rubric in this chart to help you improve your historical investigation report.

Questions	Do This	Changes You Made
1. Does the introduction draw the reader into the research, give an overview of the research, and include a thesis?	_____**Underline** the sentence that would draw in the reader. _____**Box** the overview of the research. _____**Circle** the thesis statement.	
2. Do several main ideas develop the thesis?	_____**Number** each main idea in the margin.	
3. Are the main ideas supported by facts and details?	_____**Draw an arrow** from each main idea to a fact or detail that supports it.	
4. Does the report include summaries and paraphrases as well as direct quotations?	_____**Highlight** all direct quotations. If direct quotations compose more than one-third of the report, revise.	
5. Are all sources cited when necessary? Are they formatted correctly?	_____**Put a star** next to direct quotations and facts that are not cited or correctly formatted.	
6. Does the conclusion restate the thesis, summarize the main ideas, and include a final thought?	_____**Circle** the restatement of the thesis. _____**Box** the summary of the main ideas. _____**Bracket** the thought-provoking ending.	

Proofreading Checklist

GUIDELINES FOR PROOFREADING	Yes	No	Needs Work
Is every sentence complete, not a fragment or a run-on?			
Are punctuation marks—such as end marks, commas, semicolons, colons, dashes, and quotation marks—used correctly?			
Are proper nouns, proper adjectives, and the first words of sentences capitalized?			
Does every verb agree in number with its subject?			
Are verbs and tenses used correctly?			
Are subject and object forms of personal pronouns used correctly?			
Does every pronoun agree with its antecedent in number and in gender? Are pronoun references clear?			
Are frequently confused words (such as *fewer* and *less*, *affect* and *effect*) used correctly?			
Are all words spelled correctly? Are the plural forms of words correct?			
Is the paper neat and correct in form?			

Framework for Historical Investigation Reports

Use the following framework to help you evaluate your own writing
and the models on the following pages.

- Clearly **states thesis** and provides **sound evidence** in support of that thesis
- Provides essential **background information**
- Relies on information from **multiple sources**
- **Documents sources** of information in the paper
- Uses a **formal, objective tone**
- Demonstrates effective **organization** throughout
- Offers a **thought-provoking point of view and conclusion**

Historical Investigation Report: Score Point 4

Read the student model below. With the Framework as a guide, write an evaluation of the model in the commentary box, explaining why the model received the score shown above.

Model	Commentary
In the summer of 1921, a 14-year-old Idaho farm boy named Philo T. Farnsworth had a breakthrough idea that changed the world. In an instant of gazing out across the rows of a field he was plowing, Philo "saw" how electronic television could be accomplished. This insight led Philo to dedicate his life to developing television. One powerful competitor kept Philo from getting the credit he so deserved for his invention. Nevertheless, history proves that Farnsworth was the "father of television."	
Philo's realization in the field that day was that an image could be transmitted electronically line by line. "Each line could be converted into electricity and sent over a distance. At the receiving end, the electrical units could be reassembled into the same pattern and turned back into a picture" (McPherson 265).	
Philo became the first to transmit an electronic image. That image, sent to the TV receiver he had invented, was "…a blurred line [that] split the tiny screen of the receiver" (Schwartz 88). Philo improved the clarity of the image, and by 1930, he had patents for both his television camera and receiver, and the future looked promising.	
But Philo had competitors, such as David Sarnoff, head of the powerful Radio Corporation of America. With brutal intent, Sarnoff's high-powered lawyers spent years battling Philo in court, trying to prove RCA's ownership of TV technology. Philo consistently won rights. Despite this, when the 1939 World's Fair rolled around, Philo's company had no money to exhibit its new televisions, so RCA introduced TV to the world.	
Now, decades later, Philo's crucial role is finally being recognized. Recently a statue of him was added to the National Gallery of Statuary. It reads Philo T. Farnsworth, Father of Television.	
Bibliography	
McPherson, Stephanie Sammartino. TV's Forgotten Hero: The Story of Philo T. Farnsworth. Minneapolis, MN: Carolrhoda Books, 1996.	
Schwartz, Evan I. The Last Lone Inventor: A Tale of Genius, Deceit, and the Birth of Television. New York, NY: HarperCollins, 2002.	

Historical Investigation Report: Score Point 3

Read the student model below. With the Framework as a guide, write an evaluation of the model in the commentary box, explaining why the model received the score shown above.

Model	Commentary
In the summer of 1921, 14-year-old Philo T. Farnsworth had an incredible realazation. He was plowing an Idaho field and looked back at the neat rows of earth. This gave Philo the idea that television pictures could be transmitted line by line. At that time there was no television but some people were thinking about it. Philo was the first person to ever discover the way. Even though he had stiff competition, he had an advantage. For this reason, he should be known as the Father of Television, even though most people have never even heard of him.	
During his twenties, Philo began dedicating all his time and money to inventing television. But people at the powerful Radio Corperation of America were also trying. RCA was not used to giving anything to the "little guy." David Sarnoff, the head of that company, was determined to keep Philo and his company out of the TV making game.	
Unfortunately for David Sarnoff, Philo got patents for his inventions of the TV camera and TV set before RCA did. That made RCAs lawyers spend years in court trying to beat out Philo and prove they really deserved patents too. Without there own patents, they had to pay royalties to make televisions. This was not something Sarnoff wanted to do.	
But in numerous court decisions, the judge always ruled that "priority of invention is awarded to Philo T. Farnsworth." The problem for Philo was money though. He spent so much over many years of experimenting. So even though he really was the first to transmitt an image from a camera to a TV set, he couldn't beat out RCA. When the 1939 World's Fair took place, RCA had a huge booth and lots of publicity. Everyone called them the inventors of television.	
Philo didn't even have enough money to have a booth at all. So pretty soon his name was all but forgotton. Today its coming back though. More and more people are realizing who really invented TV. Philo even has a statue in the national gallery and along with his name it says Father of Television.	

Historical Investigation Report: Score Point 2

Read the student model below. With the Framework as a guide, write an evaluation of the model in the commentary box, explaining why the model received the score shown above.

Model	Commentary
Here's something you probly don't know. A guy named Philo T. Farnsworth invented television. That's right. A 14-year-old farm boy invented TV! He didn't do it at 14 of coarse. He first got the idea how to do it then. That was when he was plowing a field in Idaho. He looked the rows of dirt he'd just plowed. That made him think of the idea to send a TV picture one line at a time. Pretty crazy! But it worked! So Philo Farnsworth was really the father of television. It didn't happen all at once though.	
Philo started working on making a television all through his twenties. He had lived in a lot of states in the west but now he was in San Francisco. He first made a thin blurry line appeer on the screen their in his lab. Then he did some focusing and the line got strait and clear. No one on the planet had did this before!	
Some big guns at RCA were also trying to invent TV at the same time. The top gun of that company was David Sarnoff. He only wanted power for himself. He wanted to make sure he got the credit for being TVs inventer. His laywers fought Philo in court. This went on for years. But Philo had a pattent for his inventions already, so they would have to pay him to make TVs to. David Sarnoff refused to do this. He was good at wearing Philo out to. This happened both in court and everywhere else. It proved you cant fight the big guys to easily!	
It took David Sarnoff a while to get what he wanted. But he finally did. That's when he went gangbusters! He left poor broke Philo in the dust. RCA had a booth the 1939 World's Fair where they showed of RCA Tvs to the world. Philo couldn't even pay to get in he was so broke! So David Sarnoff got all the invention credit. But not forever. Finnaly, a statue in Washington d.c. somewhere is of Philo. It call's him the father of television. Good move!	

Practice with Conventions

Circle the letter of the best answer to each of the following items.
(40 points; 4 points each)

1. **Which version of the sentence shows correct punctuation?**

   A) "Run while you can" screamed Tina, the expedition leader.

   B) "Run while you can!," screamed Tina, the expedition leader.

   C) "Run while you can!" screamed Tina, the expedition leader.

   D) "Run while you can"! screamed Tina, the expedition leader.

2. **Which word is spelled incorrectly?**

   A) aisle

   B) ile

   C) I'll

   D isle

3. **Which version of the sentence shows correct capitalization?**

   A) Susan p. Nelson founded Caretakers of the Forests, an Environmental group.

   B) Susan P. Nelson founded Caretakers of the Forests, an environmental group.

   C) Susan p. Nelson founded Caretakers Of The forests, an environmental group.

   D) Susan P. Nelson founded Caretakers of the Forests, an Environmental Group.

4. **Which sentence is grammatically correct?**

   A) Both Tom and Vicki think the film should be shown.

   B) Mr. Smith, Mrs. Vivas, and Ms. Green has applied for the job.

   C) One of the speeches were written by Maya Angelou, the poet.

   D) Though it may appear to be a comet, it was really a shooting star.

5. **Which version of the sentence shows correct punctuation?**

   A) Davis Electric, the sponsor, was a strong profitable, established business.

   B) Davis Electric, the sponsor, was a strong, profitable, established business.

   C) Davis Electric, the sponsor, was a strong, profitable, established, business.

   D) Davis Electric, the sponsor, was a strong profitable established business.

6. **Read this sentence.**

   > Neither the cold <u>and the wind</u> stopped the race from starting.

   How should the underlined portion be written?

   A) but the wind

   B) or the wind

   C) nor the wind

   D) plus the wind

7. Which word is spelled correctly?

A) beggar

B) calender

C) deside

D) fatige

8. Which version of the sentence shows correct capitalization?

A) They fished at Cable Lake, which is in Iron County just north of Crystal Falls.

B) They fished at Cable lake, which is in Iron county just North of Crystal falls.

C) They fished at Cable Lake, which is in iron county just north of Crystal Falls.

D) They fished at Cable Lake, which is in Iron County just North of crystal Falls.

9. Which word is spelled correctly?

A) imitasion

B) missille

C) opinion

D) recieve

10. Why would Anil use bullet points in his research paper?

A) to cite a source

B) to place information into a list

C) to increase white space in the paper

D) to tell what a section of the paper will cover

Prewriting: Reflective Composition Writing Prompts

**Choose your own experience for a reflective composition, or use one of the
following prompts to help you write a reflective composition.**

WORKPLACE

You have probably had a work experience, whether holding a full-time summer
job or merely helping a friend, that changed the way you think about others or
yourself. Write a reflective composition about the experience, and remember to use
concrete sensory details to describe the events that made up the experience. Share
the essay with a classmate who has done similar work.

SCHOOL

Has an experience at school ever caused you to draw a conclusion about life in
general? What events led you to that conclusion? Write a reflective composition
describing the experience, and focus on the connection you made between the
experience and life in general. Have a friend read your composition; maybe he or
she has drawn the same conclusion.

MUSIC

Performing with a band or choir can be an intense experience. Teamwork is critical
to success. Think of an experience you have had with your school band or choir
that has had a significant effect on you. Then, write a reflective composition
describing the experience and the significance it holds for you. Share your
composition with your band or choir director.

SCIENCE

Our understanding of the natural world has been greatly influenced by results of
scientific experiments. Flying a kite in a lightning storm helped Ben Franklin
better understand electricity. Think of an experiment you have studied or
performed that has helped you see the world in a new light. Write a reflective
composition detailing the series of events that led to your new understanding.
Share the composition with your science teacher.

HISTORY

Historical events can profoundly affect the way we think. Think of a historical
event you studied or experienced that significantly changed your perception of the
world. Then, write a reflective composition focusing on the significance the event
holds for you. Share the essay with a friend or family member who has a similar
interest in the historical event.

Prewriting: Reflect on the Experience

Use the graphic organizer below to choose your experience and reflect on its meaning. Use additional paper if necessary.

- Keeping in mind your purpose and audience, use a separate sheet of paper to list experiences that have been important in your life. Choose the one that has taught you the most about yourself or the world.

- Answer the questions below to help you reflect on the meaning of your experience. Then, write a sentence that sums up its significance.

MY EXPERIENCE

REFLECTION

Questions	Answers
What did I feel during this experience?	
What did I feel when I thought about it shortly afterward?	
How do I feel about it now?	
What did I learn about others or myself from this experience?	
How did this experience influence what I believe about people or life in general?	
How have my beliefs changed or developed since then?	

SIGNIFICANCE

Writing Workshop

Prewriting: Recalling, Recording, and Arranging Details

Use the graphic organizer below to help you organize the events and details of your experience. Use additional paper if necessary.

- List as many of the individual events that made up the experience as you can remember. List the events in **chronological order.**

- Add narrative details (actions, thoughts, feelings, dialogue) and descriptive details (appearances of people, the setting). Indicate the order you will use for the details.

- You may also want to use a separate sheet of paper to organize your events and details in a flowchart.

EVENTS AND DETAILS

Event:	Narrative details:	Descriptive details:
1.		(Circle the order you will use.) Spatial order Order of importance
2.		(Circle the order you will use.) Spatial order Order of importance
3.		(Circle the order you will use.) Spatial Order Order of importance

My Writing Workshops

Drafting: Organizing and Writing Your Composition

Complete the graphic organizer below, and use it to help you write your first
draft. Use additional paper if necessary.

INTRODUCTION

Engaging opening:
Background information:
Hint at significance:

BODY

Event 1:	Event 2:	Event 3:
Details:	Details:	Details:

CONCLUSION

Significance of experience:
Connection between the experience and life in general:

Writing Workshop

Evaluating: Student Model Think Sheet

Answer the questions below to get a better understanding of the structure of a reflective composition. Use additional paper if necessary.

- Re-read "Outside of a Horse." The notes in the margin will help you identify important elements of a reflective composition.

- As you respond to the questions, think about the use of language, the organization of information, and the strategies used for developing ideas and elaborating on them.

QUESTIONS AND RESPONSES

1. Where does the experience take place?

   _____

   _____

   _____

2. What is the main event of the experience?

   _____

   _____

   _____

3. What are some details about one of the events?

   _____

   _____

   _____

4. What is the significance of the experience?

   _____

   _____

   _____

5. Does anything else catch your interest or seem important? In what way?

   _____

   _____

   _____

Evaluating: Reflective Compositions

Use the following questions to evaluate your reflective composition or that of one of your classmates.

- Make brief notes to answer the questions.
- Rate the parts of the reflective composition. The lowest score is **1,** and the highest is **4.**
- Make at least three suggestions for improving the reflective composition.

1. How well does the introduction capture the reader's attention?

   Rating: 1 2 3 4

   Suggestion: _____

2. How well does the introduction hint at the significance of the experience?

   Rating: 1 2 3 4

   Suggestion: _____

3. Is any event not presented clearly? Does the order of events make sense?

   Rating: 1 2 3 4

   Suggestion: _____

4. What details are provided about one of the events?

   Rating: 1 2 3 4

   Suggestion: _____

5. What is the significance of the experience? What final statement is made about life in general?

   Rating: 1 2 3 4

   Suggestion: _____

6. Is the tone too formal or informal?

   Rating: 1 2 3 4

   Suggestion: _____

7. Are participial phrases and parallel structures used effectively?

   Rating: 1 2 3 4

   Suggestion: _____

Writing Workshop

Revising: Improve Your Reflective Composition

Use the rubric in this chart to help you improve your reflective composition.

QUESTIONS	DO THIS	CHANGES YOU MADE
1. Does the introduction capture the reader's attention?	_____ **Bracket** any attention-getting anecdote, question, or interesting statement.	
2. Does the introduction give a hint about the significance of the experience?	_____ **Underline** the sentence or sentences that hint at the significance of the experience.	
3. Are the specific events of the experience presented clearly and in an order that makes sense?	_____ **Number** each event, and if the events are not presented clearly or in a logical order, revise.	
4. Do narrative and descriptive details describe the people, places, and events?	_____ **Circle** the sentences that help readers imagine the people, places, and events.	
5. Does the conclusion make the significance of the experience clear? Does it include a final statement that connects the experience to life in general?	_____ **Star** the sentence that relates the meaning of the experience.	
6. Does the composition sound stuffy? Are there places where words or expressions could make it sound more informal?	_____ **Highlight** any words or expressions that seem overly formal or unnatural.	
7. Does the composition make use of participial phrases or parallel structures to advance the story or balance descriptive language?	_____ **Box** any participial phrases. _____ **Draw a wavy line** under parallel structures.	

Writing Workshop

Proofreading Checklist

GUIDELINES FOR PROOFREADING	Yes	No	Needs Work
Is every sentence complete, not a fragment or a run-on?			
Are punctuation marks—such as end marks, commas, semicolons, colons, dashes, and quotation marks—used correctly?			
Are proper nouns, proper adjectives, and the first words of sentences capitalized?			
Does every verb agree in number with its subject?			
Are verbs and tenses used correctly?			
Are subject and object forms of personal pronouns used correctly?			
Does every pronoun agree with its antecedent in number and in gender? Are pronoun references clear?			
Are frequently confused words (such as *fewer* and *less*, *affect* and *effect*) used correctly?			
Are all words spelled correctly? Are the plural forms of words correct?			
Is the paper neat and correct in form?			

Framework for Reflective Compositions

Use the following framework to help you evaluate your own writing and the models on the following pages.

- Highlights a single, **meaningful experience**
- Uses **descriptive, sensory details** to fully convey events
- Uses **narrative details** and **dialogue** to relate actions, thoughts, and feelings
- Provides a **logical, organized progression of** events
- Clearly expresses the **significance of the experience**

Reflective Composition: Score Point 4

Read the student model below. With the Framework as a guide, write an evaluation of the model in the commentary box, explaining why the model received the score shown above.

Model	Commentary
The air had a mellow warmth, but the lake water was chilly, and suddenly I knew it was my grave. Dark thoughts swarmed in on me: I'm drowning. We're not going to make it to the float. I'm dead in the water, and so is Kaneesha.	
Choking and spluttering, I fought frantically to stay above the surface, remembering how carelessly I'd agreed to swim my six-year-old half-sister to the big log float anchored out in the lake. I'd expected Kaneesha to just relax behind me with her hands lightly on my shoulders. But she'd begun to tense up as soon as we hit deep water, and now we were both in trouble.	
We were so close to the float, but it was still several frustrating feet away. Our family's summer vacation was about to come to an abrupt and awful end, that much seemed certain.	
"Kaneesha, stop it!" I cried, gasping for air. "Relax your arms!" But Kaneesha was terrified. She clung desperately to my shoulders, not listening. Her bent arms had become as rigid as thin metal rods as she attempted to keep her own head above water. Her struggle to stay up was pushing me down, literally submerging me. The cute little girl who, for me, had been the highlight of our blended family, was now my enemy. Could I save myself and still have enough energy to keep hold of Kaneesha? No, it was either her or me. Or probably neither of us.	
Suddenly, as my head came up for what I was afraid would be the last time, something firm but soft bumped against my body. An inner tube! I grabbed it like it was my last hope—because it was. I made sure Kaneesha took hold, too. I heard shouting and looked back to see a guy swimming toward us from the beach. I realized he was the one who had pushed the inner tube out to us. We were saved!	
Safely back on the beach, I hugged Kaneesha tight. I'd never been so glad we were both alive. Life was good, so good! On the edge of death, I'd learned something important. I was sixteen and pretty grown up. But I needed to do a lot more growing before I ever took responsibility for another person's life again.	

Writing Workshop

Reflective Composition: Score Point 3

Read the student model below. With the Framework as a guide, write an evaluation of the model in the commentary box, explaining why the model received the score shown above.

Model	Commentary
The warm summer air would have felt good if I wasn't about to drowne. As it was, all I could feel was the chill in the water as I spluttered and shouted for help. And I wasn't the only one who was going to drown. My six-year-old half-sister, Kaneesha, had asked me to swim her out to the big log float anchered in the lake. Now in the deep water she was just pushing me down instead of holding onto my shoulders and floating behind me like I wanted her to.	
What was I going to do? I had gotten nearer to the float, but still too far out in the lake to reach. It looked like our family vacation would be coming to a sudden, not-so-great ending. I couldn't believe I was so helpless either! But at least I had on my new bathing suit, which was better for swimming than my old one.	
"Kaneesha, stop it!" I cried, grasping for air. "Relax your arms!" But Kaneesha was terrified. She clung desparately to my shoulders, not listening. Her struggle to keep her head out of the water made her start pushing down on my shoulders like I was some life raft or something. But I wasn't. I kept going under, more like a death raft. And now, even though she was my favorite in our blended family, she was turning out to be my enemy instead, it seemed like. I was thinking I was pretty sure I couldn't save both her and me. What could I do?	
My head went under again, and just as I came back up chocking for air, something firm and rubbery bumped up against me. I couldn't believe I saw an innertube! I grabbed it instantly and just clung on. I made sure Kaneesha grabbed on, too. Then I heard shouting and looked back and saw some guy swimming toward us from the beach. We're saved, I thought!	
That innertube did save Kaneesha and me. So on the beach I didn't think of her as my enemy anymore, of course. We were both safe and alive. I was glad we were rescued, of course, because life is good. But I was mainly thinking it would be a long time before I did that again!	

Reflective Composition: Score Point 2

Read the student model below. With the Framework as a guide, write an evaluation of the model in the commentary box, explaining why the model received the score shown above.

Model	Commentary
I was on the beach early in the morning. The sun was really hot that day and water was tottally chilly. I wanted to swim out to the raft that was floating out in the lake, and I had a new bathing suit I really like on. But when my half-sister, who's name is Kaneesha, came along and wanted me to swim her out there too I figured I could do that. Kaneesha, my six-year-old half-sister doesn't swim so good. She can dog padle, but she said she promised she would just relax in the water and put her hands on my shoulders and just stay like that. But it ended up not the case. As soon as we got deeper and deeper, she started freaking out. I mean, she didn't just relax like I said. She started really pushing on my shoulders so she could stay up. But that meant she was pushing me down. My head started going underwater, which was not cool. I was swalowing water and started choking. Sometimes I choke easily just from taking a drink of water, but this was way worse than that. As I was trying not to drowned, because the float thing was still really far off, I started thinking this was a stupid idea for a family vacation. I like swimming but I didn't exacly want to drown because Kaneesha couldnt swim. Then I thought about last summer when we went to something called a dude ranch and rode horses and things like that. It was where I suddenly wished I was now. Things were getting really bad now. Kaneesha was hollering and I have to admit so was I. Then like out of the blue, I get bumped by this big black innertoob. Was that excelant or what! I grabbed that thing like it was more importent than anything else in the world, because it was right at that moment. Kaneesha grabbed on to, and pretty soon we were back on the beach. That was mainly because the guy who had pushed the innertoob out to us helped us get back to shore. That was a pretty big important day in my life to be alive and tottally O.K. I'll probly remember it for ever.	

Writing Workshop

Practice with Conventions

Circle the letter of the best answer to each of the following items.
(40 points; 4 points each)

1. **Which version of the sentence is grammatically correct?**

   A) He jumped over the fence, ran across the yard, and climbed up the tree.

   B) He jumps over the fence, ran across the yard, and climbs up the tree.

   C) He jumps over the fence, runs across the yard, and climbed up the tree.

   D) He had jumped over the fence, had ran across the yard, and climbed up the tree.

2. **How should Romario format his reflective composition?**

   A) single-spaced

   B) 1.5-spaced

   C) double-spaced

   D) triple-spaced

3. **Which version of the sentence shows correct capitalization?**

   A) Sue Tan, of Oak high school, was voted Best Artist for her parthenon model.

   B) Sue Tan, of Oak High School, was voted Best artist for her Parthenon model.

   C) Sue Tan, of Oak High School, was voted Best Artist for her Parthenon model.

   D) Sue Tan, of Oak High School, was voted Best Artist for her parthenon model.

4. **Which word is spelled correctly?**

   A) hankerchief

   B) insadent

   C) lisence

   D) neighbors

5. **Which version of the sentence shows correct punctuation?**

   A) Dr. Wilma K. Dorfman, of 112 S. Maple Blvd, will administer the shots.

   B) Dr. Wilma K. Dorfman, of 112 S. Maple Blvd., will administer the shots.

   C) Dr. Wilma K. Dorfman, of 112 S Maple Blvd., will administer the shots.

   D) Dr. Wilma K Dorfman, of 112 S. Maple Blvd, will administer the shots.

6. **Which word is spelled incorrectly?**

   A) benefited

   B) catastrofe

   C) experienced

   D) initial

7. Read this sentence.

> Pang Hu's <u>best friend, and top advisor, that's</u> Fred Walsh.

How should the underlined portion be written?

A) best friend and top advisor are

B) best friends and top advisors are

C) best friend and top advisor were

D) best friend and top advisor is

8. Which version of the sentence shows correct capitalization?

A) I asked mayor Schultz if his mother, Steffi, was at the Newman Clinic.

B) I asked Mayor Schultz if his mother, Steffi, was at the Newman Clinic.

C) I asked Mayor Schultz if his Mother, Steffi, was at the Newman Clinic.

D) I asked Mayor Schultz if his mother, Steffi, was at the Newman clinic

9. Which word is spelled correctly?

A) medecine

B) neccesary

C) potatoe

D) sufficient

10. Which version of the sentence shows correct punctuation?

A) "He won fair and square," Jim said. "What else is there to say?"

B) "He won fair and square" Jim said. "What else is there to say?"

C) "He won fair and square" Jim said. "what else is there to say?"

D) "He won fair and square," Jim said, "what else is there to say?"

Prewriting: Literary Analysis Writing Prompts

Choose your own issue for your literary analysis of a novel, or use one of the following prompts.

WORKPLACE

Think of a novel in which the main character's profession is integral to the story. What is the author trying to tell you about the character through the character's profession? How would the story change if you put the character in another very different profession? Write a literary analysis explaining what the character's work says about him or her. Present your analysis to a group of career-minded students.

SCHOOL

Select a novel that centers around events at a school. Write a literary analysis explaining how the setting affects the tone and the point of view of the story. Share your analysis with fellow students.

PSYCHOLOGY

Select a character such as Huck Finn, Reverend Dimmesdale from *The Scarlet Letter*, or another character from a novel you know. List in chronological order the actions of the character. What do the actions reveal about the character? Do the character's actions fit together, or do they contradict each other? Write an analysis of the character; be sure to include paraphrases or quotations from the text to support your analysis. Present your findings to a group of students interested in psychology.

SCIENCE

Physicists think of time as a fourth dimension, coloring how we perceive the world around us. Similarly, the way time is manipulated in novels affects our perceptions of the present moment of the story. Think of a novel in which time is manipulated: Scenes may be rushed or elongated (for example, an entire novel that takes place over the course of a few hours or a battle scene that seems to flash by in mere moments), or the writer may use flashbacks to take us back in time. Write a literary analysis about how time is manipulated in a novel. Share your analysis with a science class.

HISTORY

Most novels are set in specific places and historical periods that are central to the theme of the novel—for example, *The Red Badge of Courage*, *The Grapes of Wrath*, and countless others. Select a novel that is set in a historical period familiar to you. Identify the important historical details that the writer includes to bring the novel to life, and write a literary analysis explaining how those details relate to the theme. Present your analysis to a history class.

Writing Workshop

Prewriting: Read and Analyze a Literary Work

Use the charts on these two pages to help you organize your literary analysis. Answer the questions, and jot down notes about specific passages. Use additional paper if necessary.

Title and author of novel: _____

_____

LITERARY ELEMENTS

Character: How do the important characters think, talk, and act? In what ways do their actions or attitudes change over time?	
Setting: What are the time and place of the novel? How does the setting affect the mood or the development of the plot?	
Plot: What is the central conflict, or problem, of the story? How does the outcome of the conflict relate to the theme of the story?	
Point of view: Is the story told by a first-person or a third-person narrator? What does the narrator think about the characters and the events?	

STYLISTIC DEVICES

Theme: What universal truth does the novel express about human nature, experiences, problems, or relationships? What details reflect this theme?	
Symbolism: Do any objects or elements show up repeatedly? Which (if any) person, place, or thing seems to represent an abstract idea? If so, what?	
Imagery: What feelings do sensory descriptions of people, places, events, and ideas suggest? What effects are created through the use of imagery?	
Diction: Is the author's word choice straightforward, or is the language connotative? What is the novel's tone? How does the word choice affect the tone of the story?	
Figurative language: Does the author use similes and metaphors? If so, what effects do these comparisons create?	

Prewriting: Thesis, Evidence, and Order

Use the following graphic organizer to help you write your thesis, gather evidence to support your thesis, and plan your analysis. Use additional paper if necessary.

THESIS STATEMENT

_____

_____

_____

GATHER EVIDENCE

Major point:	Major point:	Major point:
Evidence:	Evidence:	Evidence:
Elaboration:	Elaboration:	Elaboration:

Arrange your ideas (circle the best way to order your information):

        Chronological order   Order of importance

Drafting: Organizing and Writing Your Analysis

Complete the graphic organizer below, and use it to help you write your first
draft. Use additional paper if necessary.

INTRODUCTION

The novel's author and title:
Relevant background information:
Thesis statement:

BODY

Outline:

CONCLUSION

Restatement of thesis and summary of main points:
Memorable statement:

Writing Workshop

Evaluating: Student Model Think Sheet

Answer the questions below to get a better understanding of the structure of a literary analysis. Use additional paper if necessary.

- Re-read "Dysfunctional Communication." The notes in the margin will help you identify important elements of a literary analysis paper.

- As you respond to the questions, think about the use of language, the organization of information, and the strategies used for developing ideas and elaborating on them.

QUESTIONS AND RESPONSES

1. What background information provides the best context for the analysis?

    _____

    _____

    _____

2. Which major point best supports the thesis? Why?

    _____

    _____

    _____

3. Which is the best piece of elaboration? Why?

    _____

    _____

    _____

4. How successful is the writer at documenting his sources?

    _____

    _____

    _____

5. Does anything else catch your interest or seem important? In what way?

    _____

    _____

    _____

Evaluating: Literary Analyses

Use the following questions to evaluate your literary analysis or that of one of your classmates.

- Make brief notes to answer the questions.
- Rate the parts of the literary analysis. The lowest score is **1**, and the highest is **4.**
- Make at least three suggestions for improving the literary analysis.

1. Does the introduction include background information? Are the title and author of the novel included?

   Rating: 1 2 3 4

   Suggestion: _____

2. Does the thesis statement present a conclusion about the novel based on a literary element or stylistic device?

   Rating: 1 2 3 4

   Suggestion: _____

3. Do the body paragraphs develop main ideas to support the thesis statement?

   Rating: 1 2 3 4

   Suggestion: _____

4. Are the main ideas supported by evidence from the novel?

   Rating: 1 2 3 4

   Suggestion: _____

5. Are the main ideas organized effectively?

   Rating: 1 2 3 4

   Suggestion: _____

6. Does the conclusion restate the thesis, summarize the main ideas, and include a memorable statement?

   Rating: 1 2 3 4

   Suggestion: _____

Writing Workshop

Revising: Improve Your Literary Analysis

Use the rubric in this chart to help you improve your literary analysis of a novel.

Questions	Do This	Changes You Made
1. Does the introduction include background information? Are the title and author of the novel included?	_____**Draw a box** around the relevant background information. _____**Underline** the title and author of the novel.	
2. Does the thesis statement present a conclusion about the novel based on a literary element or stylistic device?	_____**Circle** the literary element or the stylistic device identified in the thesis.	
3. Do the body paragraphs develop main ideas to support the thesis statement?	_____**Label** each main idea that supports the thesis in the margin.	
4. Are the main ideas supported by evidence from the novel?	_____**Highlight** each piece of relevant evidence. If any evidence does not clearly support the main idea, revise.	
5. Are the main ideas organized effectively?	_____Chronological order: **number** the main ideas in sequence. _____Order of importance: **put a star** next to the most important point.	
6. Does the conclusion restate the thesis, summarize the main ideas, and include a memorable statement?	_____**Circle** the restatement of the thesis and the summary of the main ideas. _____**Bracket** the memorable thought.	

My Writing Workshops

Writing Workshop

Proofreading Checklist

GUIDELINES FOR PROOFREADING	Yes	No	Needs Work
Is every sentence complete, not a fragment or a run-on?			
Are punctuation marks—such as end marks, commas, semicolons, colons, dashes, and quotation marks—used correctly?			
Are proper nouns, proper adjectives, and the first words of sentences capitalized?			
Does every verb agree in number with its subject?			
Are verbs and tenses used correctly?			
Are subject and object forms of personal pronouns used correctly?			
Does every pronoun agree with its antecedent in number and in gender? Are pronoun references clear?			
Are frequently confused words (such as *fewer* and *less, affect* and *effect*) used correctly?			
Are all words spelled correctly? Are the plural forms of words correct?			
Is the paper neat and correct in form?			

Framework for Literary Analyses

Use the following framework to help you evaluate your own writing and the models on the following pages.

- Shows a grasp of the most **significant ideas** in a literary work
- Focuses on a **clear, logical conclusion** about the work based on the author's use of **literary elements** and **stylistic devices**
- **Supports** viewpoints and conclusions with **textual evidence** and **elaboration**
- Demonstrates effective **organization** throughout
- **Restates thesis** in concluding paragraph

Writing Workshop

Literary Analysis: Score Point 4

Read the student model below. With the Framework as a guide, write an evaluation of the model in the commentary box, explaining why the model received the score shown above.

Model	Commentary
One dreary November evening in Austria, a research scientist is engaged in some grisly work in his laboratory. On this night the scientist, Dr. Victor Frankenstein, succeeds in bringing to life a human body he has put together from many parts. This creature is the basis of the novel <u>Frankenstein</u>, by Mary Wollstonecraft Shelley. Shelley's novel, published in 1818, exhibits elements of both Gothic and Romantic literature. Romantic literature focuses on human emotions, the supernatural, and morbid occurrences. Gothics include dark, intense emotions and, especially, use weather to show characters' feelings. These elements recur throughout Frankenstein, particularly in the images of nature that reflect the emotions and moods of the protagonist, Doctor Frankenstein.	
<u>Frankenstein</u>—the story of a "monster" who goes on a rampage against his creator—has all of these. The "miserable monster" (43) has dull yellow eyes, yellow skin, a "shriveled complexion and straight black lips" (35). Dr. Frankenstein's horror at his creation floods him with hideous images and intense emotions. "I felt the bitterness of disappointment" (235), he says.	
Throughout the novel, descriptions of nature reflect the dark subject matter and extreme inner states of Frankenstein. Fleeing his creation, the doctor hurries on, "although drenched by the rain which poured from a black and comfortless sky" (44).	
In a time of contentment, the imagery again reflects Dr. Frankenstein's mood. Shelley writes that there was a "light breeze; the soft air just ruffled the water… and the most delightful scent of flowers and hay…" (187). But after the monster murders again, the doctor retreats to a mountain glacier. This scenery parallels Dr. Frankenstein's own feelings of desolation, brokenness, and a coldness of heart.	
Mary Shelley used many elements of both Gothic and Romantic fiction throughout her novel, the impact intensified by the constant link between inner, psychological landscapes, and the outer world. All of nature seems to mirror the demons haunting Dr. Frankenstein and the storm that has fallen upon him.	

My Writing Workshops

Literary Analysis: Score Point 3

**Read the student model below. With the Framework as a guide,
write an evaluation of the model in the commentary box,
explaining why the model received the score shown above.**

Model	Commentary
One dreary November evening in Austria, a research scientist finally succeeds in a horrible experiment. Dr. Victor Frankenstein, the scientist, brings to life a human body made of many different parts. This monster is the focus of Mary Wollstonecraft's Gothic novel <u>Frankenstein</u>. The story of Dr. Frankenstein's troubles with the monster contains elaments of Romanticism and also of Gothic novels. Some of these features include intense, dark emotions, super-natural things, and using nature to show what characters are feeling and what there moods are. The novel Frankenstein has all these things. It shows the moods of the main character, Dr. Frankenstein, in many scenes of nature especially. Today, most people think the name "Frankenstein" is the name of the monster. But in the book, this creature never has a name. Its the doctor who has this name. Some of the monster's feelings are described but the book is mainly about Dr. Frankenstein. For example, after the monster comes alive, Frankenstein says, "Mingled with this horror, I felt the bitterness of disappointment" (235) because the monster was a failure. When Frankenstein runs away from it, he becomes soaked from rain. Even later in the book, Frankenstein climbs a glacier after the monster has killed some people. Upset, he describes the scenery like his own mood: "a scene terrifically desolate…where trees lie broken and…the path…is intersected by ravines of snow" (124). Dr. Frankenstein is obviously feeling desolate and broken, too. But during a good moment, the scenery and weather are good too because there was a "light breeze; the soft air just ruffled the water… and the most delightful scent of flowers and hay…" (187). All in all, whatever Victor Frankenstein is feeling shows up clearly on the environment and weather also. This clearly shows that this is a Gothic and Romantic novel. Victor is defeated in the end and just wants to die. The author says the wind is rising "with great violence…the clouds swept across [the moon] swifter than the flight of a vulture…Suddenly a heavy storm, descended" (135). The storm is like the storm inside the main character, who doesn't have a happy ending.	

My Writing Workshops

Literary Analysis: Score Point 2

Read the student model below. With the Framework as a guide, write an evaluation of the model in the commentary box, explaining why the model received the score shown above.

Model	Commentary
<u>Frankenstein</u>, by Mary Shelley, the wife of the poet Percy Shelley, is a famous horror novel that starts out in a laboratory in Austria. There, the scientist Dr. Victor Frankenstein, is making a monster come to life. He used the parts of different human bodies to carry out his experiment. Frankenstein, which is the name of the doctor and not of the monster, whose never named, is horified by what he's make. How the doctor feels about his monster and the fact that this is mostly a lot of dark scenes shows this is a Gothic novel, which have this kind of theme. But Mary Shelley also wrote a Romantic liture novel in the same book. Romantic novels have a lot of emotions and weird things to. During the book, the monster starts killing people one after the another. When Mary Shelley started writing this, which was published in 1921, she was spending a rainy summer in Italy with her husband Percy and Lord Byron, the famous poet. Because they didn't have anything better to do, they started writing horror stories. So Frankenstein turned into a Gothic novel as time went on. The nature descriptions are often, and seem to match how the doctor is feeling. For instance: He became "drenched by the rain which poured from a black and comfortless sky" when he tried to run away from the monster. The monster is described especially frightning. It had yellow eyes and skin and a black line of a mouth. This is a good Gothic traight. But there are also some lighter scenes. When Victor Frankenstein is happy in one scene, it says there was a light breeze and soft air, and he could smell "delightful flowers and hay." In the end the story goes back to the dark side. After all the murders the monster committed, Victor tries to chase it down. He even chases him to the icy north pole, which seems a little unrealistic. But the descriptions make it sound totally realistic. This shows in the part where "a tumultuous sea rolled…" and he was "left drifting on a piece of ice." It also says he was preparing "for a hideous death." With all these things, this is obviously a Gothic and Romantic novel with a lot of nature included.	

Practice with Conventions

Circle the letter of the best answer to each of the following items.
(40 points; 4 points each)

1. Paula used *A Tale of Two Cities,* by Charles Dickens, for her response to literature paper. Which sentence shows how to correctly cite this book?

   A) "...tell wind and fire where to stop" (*A Tale of Two Cities* 344).

   B) "...tell wind and fire where to stop" (Dickens: *A Tale of Two Cities* 344).

   C) "...tell wind and fire where to stop" (Dickens 344).

   D) "...tell wind and fire where to stop" (344).

2. Which version of the sentence shows correct punctuation?

   A) As womens clubs become more popular, authors groups are declining.

   B) As womens' clubs become more popular, author's groups are declining.

   C) As women's clubs become more popular, authors' groups are declining.

   D) As womens's clubs become more popular, authors's groups are declining.

3. Which word is spelled incorrectly?

   A) permissible

   B) realize

   C) restarant

   D) tournament

4. Which sentence is grammatically correct?

   A) Its way too cold out now for Steve and Gary to start their hike.

   B) When she told me its real name, I almost laughed out loud.

   C) If you ask me, its going to be a long, hard journey.

   D) He believes it's charger should also work for the other phone.

5. Which version of the sentence shows correct capitalization?

   A) Which New York City bridge is older, the Pulaski Bridge or the Pelham Bridge?

   B) Which New York City Bridge is older, the Pulaski Bridge or the Pelham Bridge?

   C) Which New York City bridge is older, the Pulaski bridge or the Pelham bridge?

   D) Which New York city bridge is older, the Pulaski bridge or the Pelham bridge?

6. Which word is spelled correctly?

   A) complection

   B) eligible

   C) lonliness

   D) reccomend

7. Read this sentence.

> Marshall plans to cut the grass, <u>the garage will be organized</u>, and wash the windows.

How should the underlined portion be written?

A) garage will be organized

B) the garage organized

C) organize the garage

D) organization of the garage

8. Which version of the sentence shows correct punctuation?

A) Was it Dan Nabors who wrote the song "Lonesome Child?"

B) Was it Dan Nabors who wrote the song, "Lonesome Child"?

C) Was it Dan Nabors who wrote the song, "Lonesome Child?"

D) Was it Dan Nabors who wrote the song "Lonesome Child"?

9. Which word is spelled incorrectly?

A) backround

B) ceremony

C) definitely

D) indispensable

10. Which version of the sentence shows correct capitalization?

A) The Roman rockets basketball team has Greek, Italian, and German players.

B) The Roman Rockets Basketball Team has greek, italian, and german players.

C) The Roman rockets basketball team has Greek, Italian, and German Players.

D) The Roman Rockets basketball team has Greek, Italian, and German players.

My Writing Workshops

Prewriting: Biographical Narrative Writing Prompts

Choose your own topic for your biographical narrative, or use one of the following prompts.

WORKPLACE

Within a community there are many people who work to improve it. Whether they are politicians, law enforcement officers, community center volunteers, or librarians, they all impact others through their jobs. Choose a person who has had a significant impact on you or your community through his or her work, and write a biographical narrative about that person. Share your narrative with your school counselor.

SCHOOL

Foreign exchange students come to our schools not only to share their cultures, but to learn ours. They often bring different perspectives, which can have an impact on individual students or a school. They also face obstacles in order to fit into their new cultures and settings. Write a biographical narrative about a foreign exchange student who has changed your view of yourself, your school, or your culture.

ART

A mural painted over graffiti, a sculpture in your local park, a painting in a museum, and even a print on the wall in your dentist's office are all works of art. Individuals create artwork for a purpose, and each work impacts those who view it. Choose an artist whose artwork has had an impact on you, and write a biographical narrative exploring the significance of the artist and what led him or her to create the work. Share your narrative with an art teacher.

PHYSICAL EDUCATION

Individuals involved in sports are known for pushing their limits and inspiring others. Choose a person whose athletic feats have inspired you and write a biographical narrative that illustrates that person's significance to you. Perhaps it was a coach who convinced you that you could achieve something incredible. Maybe it was an athlete who defied all odds to compete, such a swimmer who swam an extraordinary distance or someone with a disability who fought his or her way to the finish line. Share your narrative with those who might also be inspired.

PSYCHOLOGY

Who has had the greatest influence on your personality and on the way you relate to others? From a young age, humans observe the behaviors and morals of those around them, and begin to shape their own behaviors based these observations. Write a biographical narrative about a person (perhaps a friend or relative) who has been instrumental in shaping who you are today.

Prewriting: Choose a Subject and Organize Your Ideas

Use the charts below to help you choose a subject and organize ideas for your biographical narrative. Use additional paper if necessary.

- Find two people who have had a significant impact on your life or the lives of others.
- Record why they are significant and two or three incidents or facts that demonstrate their significance.
- Select the person that will be the best subject for your narrative and write a statement capturing your perspective on that person's importance to you or others.
- Organize your ideas by recording incidents or facts that support your statement and listing descriptive and narrative details about each incident or fact.

People	Significance to me or others	Incidents or facts
Person 1:		
Person 2:		

Statement of subject's significance:_____

_____

_____

Incident or Fact	Detail 1	Detail 2	Detail 3
1.			
2.			
3.			

Writing Workshop

Drafting: Organizing and Writing Your Narrative

Complete the graphic organizer below, and use it to help you write your first draft. Use additional paper if necessary.

INTRODUCTION

Attention-grabber:
Background information:
Statement of significance:

BODY

First incident or fact:	Second incident or fact:	Third incident or fact:
Relationship to thesis:	Relationship to thesis:	Relationship to thesis:
Narrative and descriptive details:	Narrative and descriptive details:	Narrative and descriptive details:

Order: (Check one) _____ Chronological order _____ Order of importance

CONCLUSION

Restatement of significance:

My Writing Workshops

Writing Workshop

Evaluating: Student Model Think Sheet

Answer the questions below to get a better understanding of the structure of a biographical narrative. Use additional paper if necessary.

- Re-read "The Crucible of Friendship." The notes in the margin will help you identify important elements of a biographical narrative.

- As you respond to the questions, think about the use of language, the organization of information, and the strategies used for developing ideas and elaborating on them.

QUESTIONS AND RESPONSES

1. Who is the subject of the narrative?

   _____

   _____

   _____

2. What piece of background information is most important for the reader to know? Why?

   _____

   _____

   _____

3. Which incident had the greatest impact on the subject?

   _____

   _____

   _____

4. What narrative details are included to help the reader understand the incident?

   _____

   _____

   _____

5. How does the revision of the introduction help the audience preview what the biographical narrative will be about?

   _____

   _____

   _____

Writing Workshop

Evaluating: Biographical Narratives

Use the following questions to evaluate your biographical narrative or that of one of your classmates.

- Make brief notes to answer the questions.
- Rate the parts of the biographical narrative. The lowest score is **1,** and the highest is **4.**
- Make at least three suggestions for improving the biographical narrative.

1. How does the introduction grab the reader's attention and relate the subject's importance?

   Rating: 1   2   3   4

   Suggestion: _____

2. What incidents or facts are included to support the thesis or statement of significance?

   Rating: 1   2   3   4

   Suggestion: _____

3. What narrative and descriptive details are included?

   Rating: 1   2   3   4

   Suggestion: _____

4. How are the incidents or facts organized?

   Rating: 1   2   3   4

   Suggestion: _____

5. How well does the conclusion restate the thesis or stress the subject's significance?

   Rating: 1   2   3   4

   Suggestion: _____

Revising: Improve Your Biographical Narrative

Use the rubric in this chart to help you improve your biographical narrative.

Questions	Do This	Changes You Made
1. Does the introduction provoke interest in the subject and hint at the subject's significance?	_____**Underline** the introduction of the subject. _____**Double underline** any hint of the subject's significance.	
2. Do all facts and incidents contribute to the thesis statement and the significance of the individual?	_____**Star** each sentence that begins a separate incident or fact. Determine if they are related to the thesis.	
3. Are concrete sensory details used to describe all people and places?	_____**Highlight** all sensory details.	
4. Are incidents and facts organized both logically and sequentially?	_____**Number** the incidents.	
5. Does the essay contain transitions to link the incidents and facts effectively?	_____**Bracket** the transitional statements that link the incidents and facts to make a coherent whole.	
6. Does the conclusion reinforce the individual's significance and support the thesis?	_____**Box** sentences that add to the significance of the subject.	

Proofreading Checklist

GUIDELINES FOR PROOFREADING	Yes	No	Needs Work
Is every sentence complete, not a fragment or a run-on?			
Are punctuation marks—such as end marks, commas, semicolons, colons, dashes, and quotation marks—used correctly?			
Are proper nouns, proper adjectives, and the first words of sentences capitalized?			
Does every verb agree in number with its subject?			
Are verbs and tenses used correctly?			
Are subject and object forms of personal pronouns used correctly?			
Does every pronoun agree with its antecedent in number and in gender? Are pronoun references clear?			
Are frequently confused words (such as *fewer* and *less, affect* and *effect*) used correctly?			
Are all words spelled correctly? Are the plural forms of words correct?			
Is the paper neat and correct in form?			

Framework for Biographical Narratives

**Use the following framework to help you evaluate your own writing
and the models on the following pages.**

- **Focuses on an individual** well-known through research or personal experience
- **Provides essential context** or important **background information**
- Relates a **sequence of events** in the individual's life and **shows the relevance of these events**
- Conveys a **focused impression** of the individual
- **Uses concrete narrative details** and **sensory details** to ground scenes and incidents within the narrative
- **Explains the significance** of the individual

Writing Workshop

Biographical Narrative: Score Point 4

Read the student model below. With the Framework as a guide, write an evaluation of the model in the commentary box, explaining why the model received the score shown above.

Model	Commentary
Outside of those who study ancient Egyptian civilization, the name Hatshepsut is not that well known. But it should be. Hatshepsut was a remarkable ruler in a long line of Egyptian kings, called pharaohs. This pharaoh came to power about 1473 B.C. and ruled for 22 years, longer than the recorded reigns of most pharaohs. Hatshepsut is known for ruling in a time of peace, prosperity, and exploration, and for overseeing great innovative works. One of the finest of these was a magnificent mortuary temple called Djeser-Djeseru. Its awe-inspiring design was unlike any ever seen before it.	
These things together made Hatshepsut an exceptional pharaoh. But there was something even more exceptional about this ruler. Hatshepsut was a woman. In this civilization's male-dominated ruling class, this was practically unheard of. In fact, no other woman is known to have been ancient Egypt's leader for so long. And there are few traces that any other Egyptian woman ever dared to call herself king. No evidence exists that any woman ever depicted herself in traditional male pharaoh attire either. But on hundreds of the temples and structures Hatshepsut left behind she can be seen wearing male pharaoh's clothing, the royal headdress, and even a pharaoh's false beard.	
As the ruler of all Egypt, Hatshepsut erected some of the largest monuments ever seen. She oversaw an exploratory voyage to the mysterious land of Punt, from where her soldiers brought back many exotic goods. Some records even indicate that Hatshepsut herself fought in battles to keep her country safe from invaders.	
But a strange thing happened about 20 years after Hatshepsut's death. Her male successor, Thutmose III, tried to wipe out all traces of her kingship. Many of her statues were destroyed. Inscriptions with her name were wiped out. No one today knows why for sure. But modern Egyptologists think it was because the male pharaohs didn't want history recording the successful rule of a woman. They wanted things to go back to the way they had always been. But Hatshepsut's name was too great to be forgotten. Today she is still considered one of ancient Egypt's most important pharaohs.	

Biographical Narrative: Score Point 3

Read the student model below. With the Framework as a guide, write an evaluation of the model in the commentary box, explaining why the model received the score shown above.

Model	Commentary
Except for those who study ancient Egypt, the name Hatshepsut is not that well known. But it should be. Hatshepsut was one of ancient Egypt's kings, called pharoahs. This pharaoh ruled for 22 years, beginning in about 1473 B.C. This was longer than most pharaohs ruled. Hatshepsut is known for ruling in a time of peace, prosperity, and exploration. This pharaoh also built many great works, including a beautiful mortuary temple unlike any ever seen before. These things all made Hatshepsut a remarkable leader. But the most remarkable thing was that she was a woman, while normally Egyptian pharaohs were men. Like the men, Hatshepsut wore traditional male pharaoh attire, including a royal headdress and a false pharaoh's beard. No other woman is known to have had the nerve to do this. As a ruler, Hatshepsut erected some of the largest monuments ever seen. She also had an exploratory trip to the mysterious land of Punt. Her soldiers bought back incense trees, animals, and other goods from there. Some people beleive Hatshepsut even fought in battles. But a strange thing happened about 20 years after Hatshepsut's death. Her male successer, named Thutmose III, tried to wipe out all traces of her kingship. Many of her statues were hacked up and pictures of her were wiped out, along with places where her name appeared. All of this probably happened because the male pharaohs didn't want anyone to remember that there was once a great female king. They wanted it to keep on being only male kings. But unfortunately, they couldn't keep her hidden. People began to find traces of her that hadn't been destroyed. Today, Hatshepsut's name is still one of the great pharaohs of ancient Egypt.	

Biographical Narrative: Score Point 2

Read the student model below. With the Framework as a guide, write an evaluation of the model in the commentary box, explaining why the model received the score shown above.

Model	Commentary
If you haven't studied ancient Egypt, you probably havent heard the name Hatshepsut. But you should. Hatshepsut was one of the anceint Egyptian pharaohs. This pharaoh came to power about 1473 B.C. and ruled for 22 years. Very few pharaohs ever ruled as long.	
Hatshepsut was king in a peaceful time and did a lot of exploring too. The pharaoh also had many great buildings erected, such as a beutiful temple and other buildings. These are only a few remarkable things about Hatshepsut. The most remarkable thing about this pharaoh is that she wasn't a man, as you might expect. She was a woman.	
Whether or not there were other female kings in anceint Egypt is hard to say. But there's no record of any wearing the usual male pharaoh atire such as the fake beard that pharaoh's wore. Hatshepsut did wear this and other things the kings usually wore.	
Some of the other things Hatshepsut did was have her soldiers go to the land of Punt. No one knows where that was but they brought back trees and animals and other goods. This seems like it made her famous.	
But the kings that came after Hatshepsut did something strange. About 20 years after she died, they tried to get rid of her memery. They hacked up her statues and writings about her. Obviously they didn't want people later on to know there was once a female pharaoh. They wanted to get remembered for things Hatshepsut did herself. But it didn't work. Everyone knows now that Hatshepsut really did those things and that she was one of the greatest pharoahs of all.	

Practice with Conventions

Circle the letter of the best answer to each of the following items.
(40 points; 4 points each)

1. **Which sentence shows correct punctuation?**

   A) The film "There Will be Blood" is based on the novel "Oil!"

   B) After reading *Mario's Gold*, Shelly saw the film version, *Golden Man*.

   C) He thought the film "The Only One" was similar to the novel *Only This*.

   D) The novel "Mr. Math" was the basis for the film *Numbers Genius*.

2. **Which word is spelled incorrectly?**

   A) begginning

   B) conscience

   C) inconvenience

   D privilege

3. **Which version of the sentence shows correct capitalization?**

   A) Doesn't Route 13 wind down the East Coast through Delaware and Virginia?

   B) Doesn't route 13 wind down the East Coast through Delaware and Virginia?

   C) Doesn't Route 13 wind down the east Coast through Delaware and Virginia?

   D) Doesn't route 13 wind down the East coast through Delaware and Virginia?

4. **Read this sentence.**

   > The real danger <u>is begin to surface</u> months later when the dam weakened.

   How should the underlined portion be written?

   A) begun to surface

   B) is beginning to surface

   C) began to surface

   D) had began to surface

5. **Which word is spelled correctly?**

   A) ocasionally

   B) occasionally

   C) ocassionally

   D) occassionally

6. **Which version of the sentence shows correct punctuation?**

   A) Senator Guerrero stated it clearly: No more budget deficits.

   B) Senator Guerrero stated it clearly: no more budget deficits.

   C) Senator Guerrero stated it clearly; No more budget deficits.

   D) Senator Guerrero stated it clearly; no more budget deficits.

7. **Which word is spelled incorrectly?**

A) concentrate

B) likelihood

C) maintainance

D) transferred

8. **Which sentence is grammatically correct?**

A) Luisa had drank all of the grape juice in her cup.

B) I have shook the water out of my boots twice today.

C) Doris swum all the way across the small pond today.

D) Bees have attacked some animals in our county this year.

9. **Which version of the sentence shows correct capitalization?**

A) Warner, inc., published Dora's favorite play, *Long Days Of Winter*.

B) Warner, Inc., published Dora's Favorite Play, *Long Days of Winter*.

C) Warner, Inc., published Dora's favorite play, *Long Days of Winter*.

D) Warner, inc., published Dora's favorite play, *Long Days of Winter*.

10. **When would Carla use small caps in her essay?**

A) to cite the sources she used

B) to draw attention to the essay title

C) to write abbreviations of times and dates

D) to make parts of her essay more dramatic

My Presentations

Presenting and Evaluating Speeches

Complete these steps to adapt your editorial and to practice and present your speech. Cross off each step in the process as you complete it.

1. **Make your introduction dramatic.** Consider using a thought-provoking literary quotation, a touching anecdote, or a reference to an authority on the subject of your speech. State your perspective in a strong opinion statement.

2. **Choose the most effective reasons from your written editorial to present in the body of your speech.** Consider your audience and your time limitations as you choose which reasons to include.

3. **Base your arguments on logic and reason.** Avoid using logical fallacies and propaganda techniques.

4. **Organize your speech.** Make sure your speech is coherent and focused. Use one of the following approaches to organize your speech.
   - deductive reasoning
   - inductive reasoning

5. **Use some of the same rhetorical devices you used in your written editorial.**
   - repetition
   - parallelism
   - rhetorical questions
   - argument by analogy

6. **Find places where you can use irony for effect.** Make sure you use tone of voice to make the irony clear to your listening audience.

7. **Frame one or more of your arguments as a syllogism.** Consider letting your audience draw the conclusion for themselves.

8. **Make your conclusion memorable.** Summarize the main points, and restate your opinion. Finally, use specific language to call the audience to action.

9. **Practice your speech until you have it memorized.** Deliver it as a formal speech. Do not use slang, colloquialisms, or contractions.

10. **Practice your speech, using verbal and nonverbal techniques.** Note on your written speech the tone, pitch, and volume you will use at various points. Also note where you will use gestures and facial expressions. You might write a note reminding yourself to make frequent eye contact with your audience.

11. **Evaluate your speech, and get feedback.** Practice in front of a mirror, or ask friends or family for suggestions.

12. **Present your persuasive speech to your class.**

Listening & Speaking Workshop

Verbal and Nonverbal Techniques

Listen as your partner delivers his or her speech.

- Evaluate your partner's use of verbal and nonverbal techniques.
- In the Comments and Suggestions section, note instances where the speaker uses the techniques effectively. Also note where the speaker can make improvements. Use an additional sheet of paper if necessary.

THE SPEAKER	YES OR NO	COMMENTS AND SUGGESTIONS
• speaks clearly and carefully		
• varies volume or tone of voice to emphasize key words or phrases		
• pauses for effect or to emphasize important points		
• makes eye contact		
• uses appropriate facial expressions		
• uses natural gestures		

My Presentations

Listening & Speaking Workshop

Use the scale below to evaluate your classmates' speeches. Write constructive comments in the box.

3 = meets the criterion

2 = meets the criterion but needs improvement

1 = does not meet the criterion

Speaker: _____

Content

- The introduction is dramatic.   **1   2   3**
- The speaker's perspective is stated in the opinion statement.   **1   2   3**
- Sound reasons and evidence support the opinion statement.   **1   2   3**
- Reasons and evidence are presented in a logical order.   **1   2   3**
- Rhetorical devices are used.   **1   2   3**
- The conclusion summarizes the main points and calls the audience to action.   **1   2   3**

Delivery

- Tone, pitch, and volume are appropriate.   **1   2   3**
- Facial expressions and gestures are effective.   **1   2   3**
- The speaker makes eye contact with the audience.   **1   2   3**

Comments

My Presentations

Listening & Speaking Workshop

Reflection

Read the Evaluation Guides that your classmates filled out in response to your speech. Then, complete this worksheet to evaluate the effectiveness of your speech and to set goals for future speeches.

Content

1. The two areas in which I received the most scores of **1** or **2**:

   _____

   _____

2. Some comments I received on how I could improve in these areas:

   _____

   _____

3. My own ideas for improving in these areas:

   _____

   _____

   _____

Delivery

1. The two areas in which I received the most scores of **1** or **2**:

   _____

   _____

2. Some comments I received on how I could improve in these areas:

   _____

   _____

3. My own ideas for improving in these areas:

   _____

   _____

   _____

Presenting a Story

Complete these steps to prepare, practice, and deliver your story. Cross off each step in the process as you complete it.

1. **Know your story.** On your own paper answer these questions:

   - Who is the speaker (or narrator)? How does he or she look, act (consider gestures and facial expressions), and speak?

   - What is the speaker's (or the narrator's) attitude toward himself or herself? toward the subject? toward the audience?

   - Are there other characters? How do they look, act, and speak?

   - What happens in the story?

   - What tone should you use? Why is this tone appropriate?

2. **Make your details vivid.** Look carefully at the sensory details you used in your story to describe different sights, sounds, and smells. Read sensory passages aloud to make sure your language will create vivid images in listeners' minds.

3. **Clarify your organization.** Review your narrative to make sure that one event clearly leads to the next.

4. **Type a reading script.** Make a typed, double-spaced copy of your story. Leave plenty of space in the margins for notes.

5. **Plan your delivery.** Decide how to use voice and body language to convey the story.

6. **Mark on your reading script.** Mark the gestures, posture, and facial expressions you will use. Mark the pauses, vocal modulations, pace, and other verbal techniques you will use.

7. **Complete these steps to practice your delivery.**

   - Read the story aloud until you know it well.

   - Practice using your voice and body language to communicate meaning.

   - Audiotape or videotape your presentation, or tell the story in front of a mirror. Note aspects of your delivery that need improvement.

   - Ask classmates, friends, or family members to evaluate your presentation.

8. **Present your story.** Remember to relax and enjoy yourself.

Listening & Speaking Workshop

Analyze Your Story

Follow the directions below to analyze your story for presentation.

1. From what point of view will the story be told? Why did you choose this point of view?

   _____

   _____

   _____

2. Describe the action or main idea of the story.

   _____

   _____

   _____

   _____

3. Describe the speaker or narrator. How old is he or she? What does he or she look like? What can you tell about the speaker's attitude toward himself or herself? toward the subject? toward the audience?

   _____

   _____

   _____

   _____

4. Describe the tone that would be appropriate for the story. For example, is it scary or happy? serious or humorous? Why is this tone appropriate?

   _____

   _____

   _____

   _____

My Presentations

Listening & Speaking Workshop

Delivery Techniques

Use the following chart to evaluate how well your peer-review partner used verbal and nonverbal techniques.

- In the Comments and Suggestions section, note instances of effective verbal and nonverbal techniques. Also note where the speaker can make improvements.

THE SPEAKER	YES OR NO	COMMENTS AND SUGGESTIONS
• speaks clearly and carefully		
• varies volume to emphasize important words		
• pauses for effect or to emphasize important words		
• uses a tone of voice that matches the speaker's voice in the story		
• makes eye contact		
• uses appropriate facial expressions and natural gestures		

Listening & Speaking Workshop

Use the scale below to evaluate the presentations of your classmates. Then, write constructive comments for the speaker in the box below.

3 = meets the criterion

2 = meets the criterion but needs improvement

1 = does not meet the criterion

Speaker: _____

Content

• Speaker used vivid sensory details to describe sights, smells, and sounds.	1	2	3
• Transitional words and phrases help listeners follow the story events.	1	2	3
• Dialogue is effective and each speaker's identity is clear.	1	2	3
• Point of view is clear and consistent.	1	2	3

Delivery

• An appropriate pace is used.	1	2	3
• Words are enunciated and pronounced clearly and accurately.	1	2	3
• Frequent eye contact is made with the audience.	1	2	3
• Voice modulation is used to emphasize certain words and phrases.	1	2	3
• The speaker's tone is appropriate for the work and the audience.	1	2	3
• Body language, such as facial expressions and gestures, enhances the meaning of the story.	1	2	3
• The presentation stays within the established time limit.	1	2	3

Comments

Listening & Speaking Workshop

Reflection

Read the Evaluation Guides that your classmates filled out in response to your story presentation. Then, complete this worksheet to evaluate the effectiveness of your presentation and to set goals for future presentations.

Content

1. The two areas in which I received the most scores of **1** or **2**:

   _____

   _____

2. Some comments I received on how I could improve in these areas:

   _____

   _____

3. My own ideas for improving in these areas:

   _____

   _____

   _____

Delivery

1. The two areas in which I received the most scores of **1** or **2**:

   _____

   _____

2. Some comments I received on how I could improve in these areas:

   _____

   _____

3. My own ideas for improving in these areas:

   _____

   _____

   _____

Presenting an Investigation Report

Complete these steps to adapt your historical investigation report for an oral presentation and to practice and deliver the presentation. Cross off each step in the process as you complete it.

1. **Shorten or lengthen your investigation report depending on the time limit set by your teacher.** Maintain a balance of primary and secondary sources that represent relevant perspectives on your topic. Be sure to cite accurately the author and source of all quotations, statistics, facts, conclusions, and judgments that are not your own.

2. **Revise your introduction for a listening audience.** If your audience is unfamiliar with your topic, provide more background information. State your thesis so that it clearly communicates your conclusions about the topic.

3. **Use a combination of rhetorical strategies to present your analysis.**

   - exposition
   - persuasion
   - narration
   - description

4. **Restate your thesis in the conclusion.** Be sure to include a summary of your main ideas.

5. **Use notecards to deliver your presentation.** Write brief notes to remind you of your thesis, the main supporting ideas, and the details you want to include. Arrange your cards in the order you will present them.

6. **Prepare your delivery.** Enhance your delivery by using a combination of verbal and nonverbal techniques.

   - tone
   - volume
   - pause
   - rate
   - eye contact
   - facial expressions
   - gestures
   - posture

7. **Rehearse your presentation until you feel confident that you know the material and that you sound natural and spontaneous.** Videotape your presentation, or ask a family member, friend, or teacher for suggestions. Use this feedback to adjust your presentation.

8. **Deliver your presentation.** Remember to use standard American English.

Listening & Speaking Workshop

Nonverbal Techniques

Listen as your partner gives two deliveries of a one-minute section of his or her oral presentation.

- For the first delivery, evaluate your partner's eye contact and posture.
- For the second delivery, evaluate your partner's facial expressions and gestures.
- After each delivery, note instances where the speaker uses nonverbal techniques effectively. Also, note where the speaker should make improvements.

NONVERBAL TECHNIQUES	COMMENTS AND SUGGESTIONS
Eye contact:	
Posture:	
Facial expressions:	
Gestures:	

My Presentations

Use the scale below to evaluate your classmates' presentations. Write constructive comments in the box.

3 = meets the criterion
2 = meets the criterion but needs improvement
1 = does not meet the criterion

Speaker: _____

Content

- The introduction catches the audience's attention.   1   2   3
- The thesis is clearly stated in the introduction.   1   2   3
- Sources of information, such as quotations and statistics, are identified.   1   2   3
- A combination of exposition, persuasion, narration, and description is used.   1   2   3
- Information from all relevant perspectives is included.   1   2   3
- The thesis is restated in the conclusion.   1   2   3

Delivery

- Standard American English is used.   1   2   3
- A formal tone is used.   1   2   3
- Volume and rate are appropriate.   1   2   3
- Pauses are used effectively.   1   2   3
- The speaker makes eye contact with the audience.   1   2   3
- Facial expressions and gestures are appropriate.   1   2   3
- Posture conveys confidence.   1   2   3

Comments

Listening & Speaking Workshop

Reflection

Read the Evaluation Guides that your classmates filled out in response to your presentation. Then, complete this worksheet to evaluate the effectiveness of your presentation and to set goals for future presentations.

Content

1. The two areas in which I received the most scores of **1** or **2**:

   _____

   _____

2. Some comments I received on how I could improve in these areas:

   _____

   _____

3. My own ideas for improving in these areas:

   _____

   _____

   _____

Delivery

1. The two areas in which I received the most scores of **1** or **2**:

   _____

   _____

2. Some comments I received on how I could improve in these areas:

   _____

   _____

3. My own ideas for improving in these areas:

   _____

   _____

   _____

Presenting a Reflective Composition

Complete these steps to adapt your reflective composition and present it as an oral presentation. Cross off each step in the process as you complete it.

1. **Bring your reflective composition to life.** Act out, rather than describe, actions or appearances. Use dialogue to capture your characters' unique voices.

2. **Use visual and sound effects, such as props, graphics, and music, to enhance your presentation.** Be careful not to overwhelm your audience with too many effects. Choose the most effective moments to use them.

3. **Strike a balance between showing events and expressing their meaning.** Relate events in chronological order.

4. **Use clear, forceful, interesting language to engage your audience.** Check that you use the following techniques:
   - concrete images
   - figurative language

5. **Create notecards.** Write down only one event on each card. Add brief notes about any visual or sound effects, dialogue, actions, or thoughts you will use to describe the event. Arrange and number the cards in the order you will present them.

6. **Use verbal and nonverbal techniques to bring your presentation to life.** Tailor your delivery to your audience and purpose.
   - Use standard American English, except when informal expressions are used for effect.
   - Vary the volume and tone of your voice.
   - Make eye contact with the audience.
   - Use natural gestures and facial expressions.

7. **Practice your presentation, and get feedback.** Be sure to practice using your visual and sound effects.
   - Rehearse in front of a mirror. Check that your gestures and facial expressions are natural.
   - Rehearse for family or friends. Ask them for both compliments on what you've done well and suggestions on how to improve.
   - Videotape your rehearsal. Critically view the video, and take notes on where you need to improve.

8. **Present your reflection to your class.** Allow your voice and body to express your emotions and bring your experience to life.

Listening & Speaking Workshop

Adapting

Complete this Think Sheet to practice adapting a written reflection for an oral presentation.

- First, read the excerpt below from a sample written reflection.
- Then, answer the questions to adapt the reflection for oral presentation.
- Finally, use the questions to help you adapt your own reflection for oral presentation.

> We got to the swimming pool early in the morning, but it was already crowded with people. After finding a space to spread our towels, we made our way across the hot concrete to the pool. We swam for a while and then wandered over to the juice stand for some fresh lemonade. I had just taken a sip of lemonade when I spotted Susie Watchman, the meanest girl in sixth grade.

1. What **concrete imagery** could the speaker use? Write one image for each of the five senses— seeing, hearing, smelling, tasting, and touching.

   _____

   _____

   _____

   _____

2. What **figurative language,** such as a simile or a metaphor, could the speaker use?

   _____

   _____

3. What **dialogue** could be added to the presentation?

   _____

   _____

4. What **verbal** and **nonverbal techniques** could the speaker use to enliven the presentation?

   _____

   _____

5. What types of **visual** or **sound effects** could the speaker use to enhance the presentation?

   _____

   _____

Listening & Speaking Workshop

Use the scale below to evaluate your classmates' presentations. Write constructive comments in the box.

3 = meets the criterion

2 = meets the criterion but needs improvement

1 = does not meet the criterion

Speaker: _____

Content

• Key events are acted out rather than just described.	1	2	3
• Dialogue is used effectively.	1	2	3
• The importance of the experience is related.	1	2	3
• Events are presented chronologically.	1	2	3
• Concrete images, if used, are effective.	1	2	3
• Figurative language, if used, is effective.	1	2	3
• Visual and sound effects are effective.	1	2	3

Delivery

• Standard American English is used, except when informal expressions are used for effect.	1	2	3
• The speaker makes eye contact with the audience.	1	2	3
• Tone is appropriate.	1	2	3
• Volume is appropriate.	1	2	3
• Facial expressions and gestures are effective.	1	2	3

Comments

Listening & Speaking Workshop

Reflection

Read the Evaluation Guides that your classmates filled out in response to your presentation. Then, complete this worksheet to evaluate the effectiveness of your presentation and to set goals for future presentations.

Content

1. The two areas in which I received the most scores of **1** or **2**:

   _____

   _____

2. Some comments I received on how I could improve in these areas:

   _____

   _____

3. My own ideas for improving in these areas:

   _____

   _____

   _____

Delivery

1. The two areas in which I received the most scores of **1** or **2**:

   _____

   _____

2. Some comments I received on how I could improve in these areas:

   _____

   _____

3. My own ideas for improving in these areas:

   _____

   _____

   _____

My Presentations

Presenting a Literary Analysis

Complete these steps to adapt your written analysis and to practice and deliver your presentation. Cross off each step in the process as you complete it.

1. **Adapt your written thesis statement for a listening audience.**
   - Shorten and simplify your thesis statement.
   - Summarize your points in your introduction.

2. **Focus on major points that will most interest your audience.** See if you need additional points to support your new thesis. Consider the following:
   - universal themes
   - stylistic devices, such as imagery
   - other unique aspects of the text

3. **Support each major point with accurate and detailed references to the text or to other works.** If appropriate, elaborate on the evidence by discussing any ambiguities, nuances, or complexities.

4. **Try using rhetorical strategies to make your presentation easier for listeners to understand and remember.**
   - Ask a rhetorical question for effect.
   - Use parallel structure for similar ideas.

5. **Add clue words that indicate the order you are using for your oral presentation.**
   - Use *first*, *then*, and *finally* for chronological order.
   - Use *for one thing*, *further*, and *most important* for order of importance.

6. **Make brief notes on notecards.** Number the cards in the order in which you plan to use them.

7. **Rehearse your presentation.** Practice using verbal techniques, such as volume and tone, and nonverbal techniques, such as gestures and facial expressions. Try using these rehearsal strategies:
   - Videotape or audiotape your presentation.
   - Practice in front of a mirror.
   - Give your presentation to friends or family members, and ask for feedback.

8. **Present your analysis to your class.** Ask for feedback on your presentation.

Introductions and Conclusions

Complete this Think Sheet. Then, ask a partner to help you choose the most interesting way to begin and end your oral presentation.

Introduction
Use one of these techniques to grab the audience's attention.

- Write a statement that connects the novel to the listeners' lives.

_____

_____

- Write a rhetorical question you might ask.

_____

_____

- Write a compelling quotation from the novel.

_____

_____

Conclusion
Use one of these techniques to offer final insight into your topic.

- Write a thought or an observation that will prompt the audience to think further about the novel.

_____

_____

- Write a statement that shows your appreciation of the author or the novel.

_____

_____

Use the scale below to evaluate your classmates' presentations. Write constructive comments in the box.

3 = meets the criterion
2 = meets the criterion but needs improvement
1 = does not meet the criterion

Speaker: _____

Content

- Thesis statement is short and clear, yet it still shows a comprehensive understanding of the significant ideas in the novel. **1   2   3**
- Major points are summarized in the introduction. **1   2   3**
- Major points are supported by accurate and detailed references to the work. **1   2   3**
- Rhetorical strategies are used effectively. **1   2   3**
- A coherent and logical order is used. **1   2   3**

Delivery

- Volume and tone are appropriate. **1   2   3**
- Facial expressions are appropriate. **1   2   3**
- Eye contact is made with the audience. **1   2   3**
- Voice and gestures emphasize important ideas. **1   2   3**

Comments

Listening & Speaking Workshop

Reflection

Read the Evaluation Guides that your classmates filled out in response to your presentation. Then, complete this worksheet to evaluate the effectiveness of your presentation and to set goals for future presentations.

Content

1. The two areas in which I received the most scores of **1** or **2**:

   _____

   _____

2. Some comments I received on how I could improve in these areas:

   _____

   _____

3. My own ideas for improving in these areas:

   _____

   _____

   _____

Delivery

1. The two areas in which I received the most scores of **1** or **2**:

   _____

   _____

2. Some comments I received on how I could improve in these areas:

   _____

   _____

3. My own ideas for improving in these areas:

   _____

   _____

   _____

Analyzing Media

Complete these steps to apply analytical skills to the media that surround you and to combine media into a presentation of your own. Cross off each step as you complete it.

1. **Choose a topic.** Examine as many print and electronic political advertisements as possible, and look for the propaganda methods listed below. Select the political advertisement or group of related political advertisements that most interest(s) you.

   - Ad Hominem Attack
   - Card Stacking
   - Celebrity Endorsement
   - Escape
   - Facts and Figures

   - Glittering Generalities
   - Lifestyle
   - Nonconformity
   - Peer Approval
   - Plain Folks/Snob Appeal

2. **Select text, images, and sound to convey your message.** Use text for important facts, figures, or quotations: Then gather still images, sound clips, and video clips (when available) to enhance your presentation.

3. **Consider your audience.** Think about what your audience already knows about your topic, and what they'll want to know. Then select the form of media you think your audience would find most interesting.

4. **Maximize your impact.** Select high-quality materials in text, images, and sound, and use them appropriately in your presentation. Make sure text and images are large enough for everyone in your audience to see, and sound is loud enough for your audience to hear.

5. **Develop a thesis statement.** In your statement, identify the most important persuasive strategies at work in the political advertisement you have chosen to analyze, and discuss their effectiveness.

6. **Organize your presentation.** Complete these steps to ensure your presentation is easy for your audience to follow.

   - Create a single slide or screen presenting the major points of your thesis as a bulleted list.

   - Create a single slide or screen for each of the major points listed in your thesis, and plan the visual backup and textual support for each point.

   - Plan your conclusion. Consider repeating your thesis slide.

   - Plan how you will integrate words, images, and sound into your presentation.

7. **Practice your presentation.** Ask classmates, friends, or family members to evaluate your presentation and offer constructive criticism on aspects of your delivery that need improvement.

Media Workshop

Analyzing Persuasive Strategies

After you have selected your political advertisement, use this Think Sheet to help you analyze its persuasive strategies and prepare for your presentation.

1. What is your initial reaction to the political advertisement? Is it the reaction the media producer wanted?

   _____

   _____

   _____

2. Is the political advertisement effective? What is appealing about it?

   _____

   _____

   _____

3. What persuasive strategies did the producer employ? List each type, and how it is used.

PERSUASIVE STRATEGIES	
Type	**How it is used**
A.	
B.	
C.	

4. Write a one- or two-sentence thesis statement that identifies the most important persuasive strategy employed by your political advertisement or group of political advertisements.

   _____

   _____

   _____

5. List at least three key points you will cover in your presentation to support your thesis statement.

_____

_____

_____

_____

_____

6. Identify the content within your presentation that will satisfy the three elements of a multimedia presentation and how you will present it.

MULTIMEDIA ELEMENTS		
Media	**Content**	**Format**
Text		
Images		
Sound		

7. Write your conclusion.

_____

_____

_____

_____

_____

_____

My Presentations

Media Workshop

Use the scale below to evaluate your classmates' presentations. Write constructive comments in the box.

3 = meets the criterion

2 = meets the criterion but needs improvement

1 = does not meet the criterion

Speaker: _____

Content

• The presentation effectively blends spoken words with images and sound elements.	1 2 3
• The images and sounds used are of high quality and are clear to the audience.	1 2 3
• The needs of the audience are taken into account.	1 2 3
• The thesis is clear and supported with evidence.	1 2 3
• Information and ideas are organized in a logical way.	1 2 3
• The creator of the message and his or her purpose are considered.	1 2 3

Delivery

• Interest in and enthusiasm for the topic is expressed.	1 2 3
• Speaker is confident.	1 2 3
• Words are enunciated and pronounced clearly and accurately.	1 2 3
• Pauses are natural and not vocalized.	1 2 3
• Nonverbal behavior, such as eye contact, facial expressions, and gestures, are appropriate and effective.	1 2 3

Comments

My Presentations

Media Workshop

Reflection

Read the Evaluation Guides that your classmates filled out in response to your multimedia presentation. Then, complete this worksheet to evaluate the effectiveness of your presentation and to set goals for future presentations.

Content

1. The two areas in which I received the most scores of **1** or **2**:

   _____

   _____

2. Some comments I received on how I could improve in these areas:

   _____

   _____

3. My own ideas for improving in these areas:

   _____

   _____

   _____

Delivery

1. The two areas in which I received the most scores of **1** or **2**:

   _____

   _____

2. Some comments I received on how I could improve in these areas:

   _____

   _____

3. My own ideas for improving in these areas:

   _____

   _____

My Presentations